Saracen Chivalry

Saracen Chivalry

Counsels *on* Valor, Generosity *and the* Mystical Quest

Pir Zia Inayat-Khan

Suluk Press
Omega Publications Inc.
New Lebanon New York

Published by
OMEGA PUBLICATIONS INC.
New Lebanon NY
www.omegapub.com

Cover images courtesy of Dover Publications, Inc.
and Shutterstock.com
Calligraphy courtesy of Shutterstock.com
Cover design by Sandra Lillydahl

This edition is printed on acid-free paper that meets ANSI
standard X39–48.

Inayat-Khan, Zia (1971–)
Saracen Chivalry
Counsels on Valor, Generosity and the Mystical Quest
Includes introduction, notes and sources, glossary
1.Sufism
I. Inayat-Khan, Zia II.Title

Library of Congress Control Number: 2012943565

Printed and bound in the United States of America
by Sheridan Books Inc., Ann Arbor Michigan

ISBN 978–0930872915 (paper)
ISBN 978–0930872939 (cloth)

Contents

Tabarruk

WITH great gladness of heart, I invoke blessings upon this splendid book and its author, my dear nephew Pir Zia. May Queen Belacane's wisdom revive the age-old, life-giving union of mysticism and chivalry, which is so needed in our time. For a future brightened by the knightly virtues of valor and generosity, let us say, with the Andalusians, *"ojalá"*: God willing!

Shaikh al-Mashaik Mahmood Khan
The Hague, July, 2012

Introduction

IN THE annals of valor, courtesy and courtly love, Christians and Moslems figure as friends as often as foes. Harun ar-Rashid and Charlemagne might have been pillars of competing faiths, but it pleased the Caliph to send the Emperor the gift of a white elephant. For all his paradoxical fame as a hero of the Reconquista, it was in the service of a Moslem king that Don Rodrigo Diaz de Vivar earned the sobriquet El Cid. Saladin and Richard I were best of enemies, so mutually attuned in chivalry that when the Sultan saw Cœur de Lion unhorsed in the Battle of Jaffa, he quickly dispatched a pair of worthy steeds.

In the enchanted universe of medieval romance, knights-errant range freely between Christendom and Dar al-Islam. The paynim Palomydes pursues the Questing Beast through Albion, joins the company of the Round Table, and vies with Tristan for the affection of La Belle Isolde. Cousin paladins Rinaldo and Orlando fall under the spell of Angelica, a Moslem princess of Cathay, while Rinaldo's sister Bradamante plights herself to the African knight Ruggiero. The pious Tancred takes up the cross against the Saracens only to have his heart conquered by one of their warrior damsels.

Not only do heroes and heroines cross borders in the romances, sometimes the romances themselves do. Echoes of the old Persian epic *Vis and Ramin* resound distinctly in *Tristan and Iseult*. Cervantes claimed that he learned Don Quixote's history from an Arabic manuscript penned by a certain Cide Hamete Benengeli. And then there is *Parzival*.

In *Parzival*, Wolfram von Eschenbach rewrote Chrétien de Troyes' unfinished Grail romance *Perceval* with dazzling flair. But he did more: he introduced a hidden story that places the quest for the Grail in a new and different light. Wolfram's source was a Provençal poet named Kyot. Kyot in turn derived the tale from a manuscript he found cast aside in Toledo, the work of a Moorish astrologer known as Flegetanis. From Kyot and Flegetanis, Wolfram learned of Parzival's Moslem half-brother Feirefiz, and how the two brothers' reconciliation led to the attainment of the Grail. In the wake of the failed Fourth Crusade, the discovery of the Grail hero's tie of blood and destiny with a Saracen was a momentous revelation.

Wolfram begins his epic with the story of Sir Gahmuret, the younger son of King Gandin of Anjou. When the King dies, Gahmuret ventures abroad to seek his fortune. Intent on entering the service of the mightiest of rulers, he makes his way to Baghdad and accepts a commission from the Caliph. A string of exploits leads him eventually to Patelamunt, the capital the African kingdom of Zazamanc, where he finds the Queen besieged by invaders. Queen Belacane is black and beautiful and wears a massive ruby for a crown. She is not Christian, but Gahmuret regards her innocence as a natural baptism. Taking up her cause, the Angevin prince defeats the attackers, winning in the end the Queen's hand and the kingship of both Zazamanc and Azagouc.

Despite his love for Belacane, who is soon with child, Gahmuret becomes restless and craves adventure. Slipping out in the night, he bids his wife farewell in a letter in which he entreats her to inform their expected son of his Angevin lineage. He does not return, and Belacane dies of sorrow.

Gahmuret's peregrinations take him to Waleis, where he marries again. His second wife is Queen Herzeloyde, granddaughter of the Grail King Titurel. Herzeloyde conceives a child, but learning that the Caliph is under siege, Gahmuret races off to his defense. In the battle for Baghdad, Gahmuret loses his life and is mourned by the Caliph as a Christian whose death is "a grief to Saracens." Shattered, Herzeloyde withdraws to the forest and raises her son Parzival in ignorance of chivalry.

As Parzival reaches the threshold of manhood he becomes aware of the existence of knights and sets out to join their ranks. In the adventures that follow he learns of his ancestry, undergoes knightly training, rescues and marries a maiden named Condwiramurs, and is admitted to the Round Table. At the enchanted castle Munsalvaesche, Parzival is shown the Grail, the "perfection of Paradise, both root and branch," but fails to ask the necessary question and loses the chance to heal its guardian, the Fisher King Anfortas, and thereby to heal the kingdom of Terre de Salvaesche. For the next four and a half years, Parzival wanders in anguish in search of a second chance.

At last, a fateful encounter opens the way. Parzival happens across a magnificently arrayed Saracen in a forest glade and at once the two knights fall into combat. The fighters prove evenly matched as they leap and thrust, their swords whooshing and clanging. Finally Parzival delivers a crashing blow to the Saracen's helmet and his sword breaks in pieces. Now the stranger shows his quality. Rather than pressing his advantage, he offers a truce, and the two knights sit down on the grassy sward. The Saracen baffles Parzival by introducing himself as Feirefiz *the Angevin*, but the mystery is solved when he removes his helmet and reveals his parti-colored complexion, "like a parchment with writing all over it, black and white all mixed up." At once Parzival perceives that this is his father's elder son.

The two brothers are overwhelmed with joy at their meeting, though Feirefiz is grieved to learn of the death of their father, whom he had come in search of. Together they make their way to King Arthur's court, where Feirefiz is received with honor and invited to the Round Table. In the midst of the ensuing celebrations, the sorceress Cundrie arrives and announces that Parzival is to become the Lord of the Grail.

Parzival and Feirefiz ride with Cundrie to Munsalvaesche. On arrival, Templars greet them and escort them to the presence of the ailing king Anfortas. This time Parzival asks the right question: *Uncle, what is it that troubles you?* Anfortas immediately regains his health, and Parzival is acclaimed the new Grail King. The Grail is brought out in a radiant and sumptuous procession, and Feirefiz falls in love with its bearer, the maiden queen Repanse de Schoye. Feirefiz accepts baptism—here we may justifiably suspect Kyot or Wolfram of wishful embroidery—and with the blessings of Anfortas and Parzival, he and Repanse de Schoye are married and depart together for the East. In India a son is born to them. His name is John—Prester John.

In *Parzival* creed matters, but deeds matter more. The chivalric code of honor transcends religious confession and unites Christians and Saracens in a commonwealth of courtesy and conscience. Though divided by belief, Parzival and Feirefiz are brothers in blood as well as spirit, as Wolfram makes clear: "these pure men without flaw each bore the heart of the other, and in their strangeness to each other they were still intimate enough."

It was a stroke of immense good fortune that Kyot chanced to salvage Flegetanis' manuscript from a heap of refuse. How many scrolls and codices, brimming with weighty lore, have been left to molder away or burn to cinders? How much of the wisdom of the ages has vanished into the hungry mouths of insects?

Sometimes lost books reappear. The book you hold in your hands, for example. Wolfram knew nothing of it, though it would have greatly intrigued him. Flegetanis knew it only by report. This little-known treatise is Queen Belacane's testament to Feirefiz. As long as he lived, Feirefiz guarded it as his most prized possession. Prester John inherited it and bequeathed it to his descendants. In time it was lost to fire, so that only its memory remained, until that too faded and was forgotten.

Now it has reappeared. Kindly do not press me for an explanation. Suffice it to say that no word that has ever been written is truly lost—if one knows where to find it. *Wa Allahu a'lam.*

A Note on Pronouns

ALTHOUGH theologians acknowledge Allah's transcendence of the limitations of gender, it is conventional in Islamic discourse—as it is in Jewish and Christian practice—to refer to God by the masculine pronoun. Nonetheless, in her counsels Queen Belacane uses masculine and feminine pronouns alternately. In this choice she is supported by Sayyid Muhammad Husayni Gisudaraz (d. 1422), an eminent saint of the Chishti Order, who asserts in his *Wujud al-'ashiqin*, "If anyone asks how the feminine pronoun (*hiyya*) can bear a likeness to God, the answer is that on the Night of the Ascension, the emanations of God the Glorified and Exalted that appeared to the Lord of the World, peace and blessings be upon him, were in feminine form."

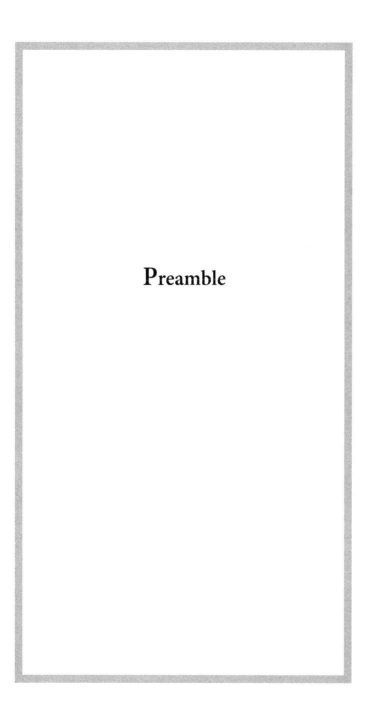

Preamble

In the Name of God,
the Merciful and Compassionate

P RAISE be to the Lord of Heaven and Earth, and peace and benedictions be upon the Prophet and his Family and Companions.

Fils du roi Gahmuret, when you read these words I will be gone. Already my body is failing. My vision grows dim, my pulses are weak, my grasp falters. I have little time left. Your father's going has torn me apart. Before he took possession of my heart I was the proudest of queens, needful of nothing and no one. Look at me now, the mere husk of who I once was. They say that love, *'ishq*, takes its name from the *'ashiqa*, a creeping vine that winds itself around a leafy tree. It climbs higher and higher, tightening its grip, drinking the tree's sap, consuming its life, un-til at last the poor tree expires. I know of what they speak. Love has killed me.

And yet, whatever the cost, I would not trade the fleeting weeks that I shared with your father for a life-time of good health and peace of mind. Ibn Gandin was—and is, wherever he may be now—the noblest of men, the very flower of chivalry and mirror of knighthood. Good blood flows in your veins.

Know, my son, that your father's father was the king of Anjou. His name was Gandin, and he died honorably in battle. King Gandin's father Addanz died in like fashion. He was first cousin to Uther Pendragon, father of Arthur. The grandfather of Addanz and Uther was Mazadan, and their grandmother was a fairy named Terdelaschoye.

Your father's line is noble, but do not forget, so too is mine. The royal house of Zazamanc is descended from King Menelik—Ibn al-Hakim—whose father was Sulayman, peace be upon him, and whose mother was Makeda, known among Arabs as Bilqis, the Queen of Sheba. Sulayman's father was Da'ud, peace be upon him. Makeda's mother was the genii princess 'Umayra.

Hold your head high! We are of the stock of prophets, princes, and fairies. But my son, blood is not all. Our holy Prophet said: "Do not bring me your genealogies; bring me your actions." On the Day of Judgment, the nobility that will carry weight is the nobility of the soul. Villainous princes will fall into the Fire while virtuous peasants taste the fruits of the Garden. Moral fiber is of the essence. Who will see to the education of your soul? Your father is gone, and I have not long to live. My relations will raise you—and yet I fret.

In truth, only my mind frets. The heart in my breast trusts in Allah, the best disposer of affairs. Did he not guide the baby Musa, peace be upon him, to safety on the bank of the Nile, rearing him under the aegis of his own eyes? Still, I must do my part. All the strength that is left in me I devote to you. What knowledge I possess of the way of truth, honor, justice, and largesse—in short, the way of chivalry—I will write down. These words are my legacy to you. May they be for you as a torch in the darkness.

On the Profession of Faith

*F*ILS *du roi* Gahmuret, the creed of our faith is *la ilaha illa'Llah Muhammadan rasul Allah*: There is no god but God, and Muhammad is the messenger of God. Learn these words, my son! Learn their music, and how they taste on the tongue. Learn their formal meaning, but do not rest there. Learn what they truly mean—as fully as you can grasp it.

La ilaha illa'Llah is the sum total of remembrance, the remembering of the Real. A soul drifts toward oblivion, lost in a Lethean haze, until God's name pierces its depths, stirring the recollection of a reality so vast and tremendous the universe cannot possibly contain it, though it suffuses and gives life to every particle of creation.

When the offspring of Adam, peace be upon him, were still in seed, God posed a question. From the beginning of time to its ultimate end, this question has been and will remain the only one that matters. He asked, *Am I not your Lord?* With all their heart, with all their soul, with all their might, they answered—*we* answered—*Yes, we testify!*

Our first word was *yes*: a promise and a pledge. Alas, with the passage of days and the vicissitudes of fate, entranced by form and heedless of essence, we have forgotten. We have turned our back on the Real: the one to whom we belong, as vassal to liege, as lover to beloved, as drop to ocean. Our *yes* has paled and lost its bloom. To return to the Real, we must now pass through the gates of *la*—no.

No object of worship exists but God.
No object exists but God.
No existence but God.

Shun idolatry, my son. When an idol rears its head in the sanctuary of your heart, shatter it on the rock of truth. Keep the inner space of your breast as stark and pure as the windswept sand of the desert waste. Do not yield to the temptation of seductive illusions. Do not stray from the path to chase after phantoms in the night. They will lead you nowhere but to perdition. Turn toward the eastern horizon, where the sun of the dawn of creation illuminates the morning of each rising moment. All that your eyes have ever seen, and ever will see, is the reflected radiance of that one perfect light.

That light is God. We know him—we know *her*, I might equally say—by many names: the Merciful, the Compassionate, the Ruler, the Holy, the Pacifier, the Faithful, the Guardian, the Mighty, the Compeller, the Proud, the Creator, the Capable, the Fashioner, the Forgiving, the Victorious, the Giver, the Sustainer, the Opener, the Knower, the Constrictor, the Expander, the Abaser, the Exalter, the Honorer, the Humiliator, the Hearer, the Seer, the Judge, the Just, the Subtle, the Aware, the Gentle, the Magnificent, the Pardoner, the Thankful, the Sublime, the Great, the Preserver, the Nourisher, the Reckoner, the Potent, the Generous, the Vigilant, the Answerer, the Vast, the Wise, the Loving, the Majestic, the Resurrector, the Witness, the Real, the Trustee, the Strong, the Firm, the Friend, the Praised, the Accounter, the Originator, the Restorer, the Life-giver, the Life-taker, the Living, the Standing, the Finder, the Glorious, the One, the Eternal, the Powerful, the Able, the Expediter, the Delayer, the First, the Last, the Manifest, the Hidden, the Master, the Supreme, the Good, the Absolver, the Avenger, the Forgiver, the Kind, the Possessor, the Lord of Power and Bounty, the Equitable, the Gatherer, the Rich, the Enricher, the Preventer, the Harmful, the Beneficial, the Light, the Guide, the Initiator, the Lasting, the Inheritor, the Director, and the Patient.

But of all of his names—all of her names—one is most essential: Allah. As you will know, Allah has four letters: *alif, lam, lam,* and *ha.* Alif and lam spell *al,* "the." When the lam is doubled, the specificity and singularity of what follows is intensified. Alif, lam, lam … ha. The one and only ha. And what is ha? Ha is the simplest, the purest, the most effortless of consonants: the sound of breath itself. When you call upon Allah, you call upon the breath within your breath. Your remembrance of him is his remembrance of himself in you.

My son, we belong to Allah and only to Allah. Live for him and die for him. Be his alone. Call his name in the morning and in the evening. Remember him when you stand, when you sit, and when you lie down. Wherever you turn your face, know that he is facing you. And know too that he sees through your eyes. Your glance never reaches him, but he reaches your glance, and all glances. She has always been, and ever will be, here, there, and everywhere, inside and outside everything. She is closer to you than your jugular vein. She is closer to you than your self. And yet, her essence is far beyond anything your mind could ever possibly conceive.

Kneel each morning facing Mecca. Swing your head in an arc, down to the left and up to the right, saying, *la ilaha.* Then say *illa*, dipping down from the right shoulder to the left breast. Say it with the focused strength of a lion's growl. As you reach the heart say, *Llahu*. Let the sound of God's name thrum in the inner cockles of your heart. After a time, leave off *la ilaha*, and say only *illa'Llahu*. Then leave off *illa*, and say only *Allahu*. Finally leave off *Allah,* and repeat the name of essence, *Hu*. This name is the sound of all sounds, the murmur of the infinite.

At first your head will sway and your tongue will recite but your mind will wander and your heart will doze. Do not be discouraged. If your intention is clear and firm, and if you practice faithfully each day without fail, your mind will at last draw to a center and your heart will begin to rouse. In time, God willing, your mind will attain perfect focus and your heart will awaken and open its eyes. You will be bathed in the ocean of being, an ocean without surface, floor, or shore. If you cleave to the truth of God's unity your remembrance will continue unabated all through the day and even into the night. You will see nothing, hear nothing, and know nothing without seeing, hearing, and knowing God in it.

Imam Shafi'i, God bless him, once went to a barber to have his moustache trimmed. The barber's task was made difficult by the Imam's constant recitation of God's name. He said, "Sir, please keep your lips still for a moment or they might be cut." Imam Shafi'i answered, "Better my lips be cut than they should cease their remembrance."

La ilaha illa'Llah forms the first half of the Profession; the second is *Muhammadan rasul Allah*. Our lord and master Muhammad the Chosen, peace and blessings be upon him, is the Messenger of God. The Messenger of God! My son, I trust you will learn to love and honor that title above all others. Emperors and archangels stand in awe of it.

Muhammad is the name of the complete human being. Were it not for him, God would not have created the heavens and the earth. Muhammad was a prophet when Adam was still between water and clay. In the figure of every messenger and prophet, Muhammad's shape is revealed, the shape of illumination.

As a mercy, God has sent prophets to all peoples. Some were received with honor; others were driven away with jeers and stones. The prophets all brought one message, the message that God is one. Some left books. The Tawra of Musa, peace be upon him, the Zabur of Da'ud, peace be upon him, the Injil of 'Isa, peace be upon him, and our own Holy Koran are among them. So too, I am of a mind to believe, are the scriptures of which we hear from our embassies in the East: the Avesta, the Vedas, and the Dhammapad. *God is not stingy of the Unseen.* If all of the trees became pens and all the oceans turned to ink, still revelation would not be exhausted.

Study the revealed books. Meditate on the Koran.
Recite it time and again; each time it will show
you something new. Strive first to acquaint your
tongue with the harmony of its rhythms and tones.
Pronounce each word with care. When you have
learned the music of the verses, turn your attention to
their meaning. Each one is a sign. Never imagine that
you can fully encompass the meaning of any of God's
signs; the sign will show you what you are ready to
see. Ready yourself by opening your mind. Expand
your heart and make it a vessel for revelation.

Burn frankincense and sit facing the Ka'ba. Recite
with a clear, melodious voice. Feel the words resound-
ing in your breast. Remember that God is near and
is listening. Submerge your whole awareness in the
waves of sound that pour through your voice. God
is listening and speaking. You are in the oratory of
eternity amidst an audience of angels.

The Koran is God's word; so too is Muhammad.
A'isha, may God bless her, said of him, "his character
was the Koran." What is inscribed in the Messenger's
book is embodied in the Messenger's spirit. If you
would study nobility read the book of his personality.

My son, follow in the footsteps of Muhammad,
'Isa, Musa, Ibrahim, and all the 124,000 prophets of
God, peace be upon them, who together form the
Cloud of Witnesses that watches over the world.
Make no distinction between them. All of God's
prophets are of such sublime eminence it would be
the height of presumption to measure one against another. When you name the prophets, call peace upon
them and remember their unity. In your mind's eye,

picture the whole of their number praying in unison in the City of Peace.

As you progress on your life's path, invoke the prophets and they will guide you. Follow their precepts and example; model your life on their tradition. Think, speak, and act in accord with their spirit so that their light illuminates your thoughts, words, and deeds.

No further prophets will come to enact sacred law. That office has been sealed; the last law-bearer was Muhammad. And yet the divine guidance continues to shine upon the world. Even today, the Friends of God draw close to the source and return with tidings of love and beauty. Were it not so, the world would fall to pieces.

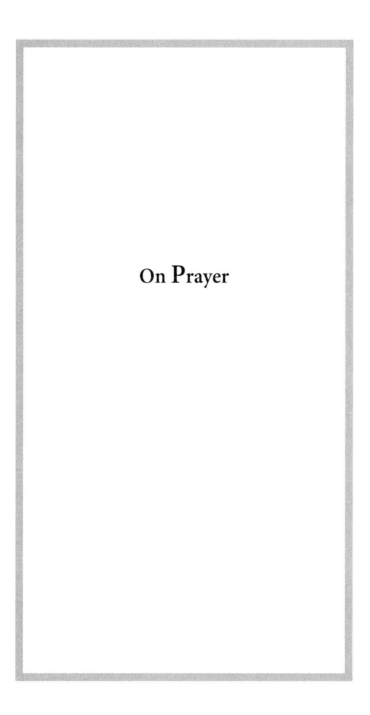

On Prayer

FILS du roi Gahmuret, prayer is ascension. When you bow down, prayer lifts you up. As your head descends to the earth, your heart ascends to the sky.

A chevalier needs a *cheval*. Palfreys and camels are commonplace; Patelamunt's streets are overcrowded with them. A real *ghazi* requires a mount of Buraq's noble breed. And what is that? The holy breath of prayer, the sigh that rises beyond time and space. Spirit rides the wind.

I trust you will perform your prayers steadfastly. Prayer is both a solemn duty and a delicate pleasure. When you step onto your prayer rug you step from the world of becoming to the world of being. When you lift your arms in praise, the burden of the past and future falls from your back and your heart expands to greet the presence of the present, which is another name for the eternal. Though you stand on earth, you bow and rise in the temple of eternity.

To pray five times each day with gesture, thought, and feeling is to put in motion the tides of a rhythm that will elevate your soul, deepen your peace, see you through danger, and guide you toward the fulfillment of your life's purpose. Hold to this rhythm when all else crumbles around you. Let dust return to dust, but prayer is heaven's portion.

The five daily prayers are a foundation. Upon this groundwork build a life of ceaseless worship. The ritual prayers follow a form. As your faith grows and ripens you will also learn to pray without form. Formless prayers follow no script. Their words arrive from, and return to, the Unseen. Sometimes they are wordless, but even then the heart's voice speaks through them.

Formless prayers are of five kinds, and the first of these is gratitude. Man dwells overlong in the gloomy shadows cast by his anxious mind. Grievances, strung together, become a tenebrous litany. Gratitude breaks the dark spell and lets light in.

Gratitude is seeing the good and giving thanks for it. The more you look for the good the more you will find it, even in what first appeared graceless. My son, the most ethereal beauty is everywhere to be seen if you know how to look. The sign that you have seen it is that your quickened spirit erupts in a hymn of praise. The more you glorify the Lord of Bounty the keener your sight will become and the more will be revealed to you. There is no limit to the splendor you will uncover if you are thankful. You need not wait for the hereafter—Rizwan will open the gates of the Garden here and now.

Sultan Mahmud was king of Ghazna at the peak of that kingdom's wealth and power. One day he called together his servants and placed valuable crystal goblets in their hands. He bade them to dash the glasses on the floor. When they did so, he thundered, "How dare you break my goblet?" They all answered,

"But, Majesty, you commanded it!" All, that is, but one. That one was ʿAyaz. His answer was, "Forgive my fault, Sire." Mahmud smiled and looked into ʿAyaz's eyes. Here was a man he believed he could trust.

Mahmud elevated ʿAyaz to the rank of Prime Minister, a position second only to the king's. The servants were astonished. The bitterest of them resolved to watch the upstart's every move in the hope of speeding his downfall. They were disappointed to find him diligent in all of his duties, but at last found promising grounds for suspicion: every day ʿAyaz quietly visited the vault of the royal treasury.

With protestations of deep regret, the jealous servants informed the king that ʿAyaz was embezzling. Mahmud answered that only the evidence of his own eyes would suffice to convict his faithful prime minister. A hole was accordingly drilled in the wall of the vault and when ʿAyaz next visited the treasury the king was furtively watching. ʿAyaz opened a chest; Mahmud held his breath.

The chest was empty except for a faded homespun robe. ʿAyaz solemnly laid aside his jeweled turban, removed his silken tunic, and donned the old robe. He stood before a mirror and spoke to his image. "'Ayaz, this is who you are: a servant. All of the glory, all of the wealth, and all of the power that you enjoy is not, in truth, your own. It belongs to His Highness. Of his boundless kindness he has favored you. Never presume. Never be haughty. Always be grateful."

As Mahmud listened, the sweetest emotion filled his breast. When ʿAyaz emerged, the Sultan embraced him and cried, "They told me you were pilfering my jewels, but I find instead that you have stolen my heart!"

The second kind of formless prayer is repentance. We aspire to great things, but time after time we fall short. We misread signs and misconstrue meanings, confusing mirages for oases. We fixate on the trivial and overlook the crucial, grasping at tinsel and trampling on truth. We mean well, but we err. Innocents are injured and our innocence is tarnished. Folly always ends in remorse.

Guilt and regret are unwelcome guests. No one wants to open her home to them. They are turned out unceremoniously—but they will not leave. They hide in the attic or basement. They lurk in the shrubs and peer through the windows at night.

Repentance means inviting them in. It means seating them, serving them tea, and hearing their story. That story will send a blush of shame to your cheeks, but it will enlighten you. You may err again, but you will not err in the same fashion.

When one has learned a lesson, suffered pangs of sore regret, and made fitting amends, what remains is to ask for forgiveness. Do not lose hope. *Do not despair of God's mercy; surely he forgives sins altogether.* God is the Merciful and Compassionate. How could he be so if we did not err? It seems that even our failures are needed in the great scheme of things. When we sin and repent, God reveals an aspect that could not otherwise be shown: his all-forgiving, all-redeeming love. He answers burning tears with healing waters.

There was once a sheikh who lived a life of continuous worship. The greater part of his day was spent in prayer, and even at night he took little rest from his devotions. One morning, however, after a long night of prostrations, the exhausted saint nearly slept through the hour of the predawn prayer. Just before the hour passed, a strange figure descended from the sky and shook him awake. You might suppose it was a guardian angel. No. It was the Accursed One.

Grateful as he was to have been awakened, the sheikh was astounded by the sight of the one who had awakened him. Answering his question before he asked it, Iblis explained: "I noticed you were on the verge of oversleeping. Had you slept too long and missed the morning prayer your grief would have been so great a tear would have dripped from your eye. So immaculate would have been the purity of that tear, it would have washed away all of the sins of the world."

The third type of formless prayer is supplication, which is to say, asking for the fulfillment of a wish. The human heart has many wants and needs, and all are not equal. Some are spiritual desires and others vain caprices. The truest desires are ofttimes the quietest; the falsest are the loudest and most insistent.

When a true desire shows itself, bring it to the one in whom desire is perfected. Whisper your want to her. The Omniscient already knows all that you think and feel; yet it is a discourtesy not to address her directly. Address her, beseech her, but do not idly presume on her aid. Justify your prayer with action. If you lack the will to strive, to struggle, and to sacrifice for the attainment of your object, to disturb the peace of Providence is an impertinence.

Effort and sacrifice are necessary, but they are not sufficient. What suffices is God's will. Since that will is inscrutable, hope must be tempered with resignation. Summon up the full force of your desire. Dream in vivid colors. Act on your prayer with unwavering resolve. But in the end submit the whole matter to God, without expectation. Make your motto, "Thy will be done."

When that which you seek and the Power from whom you seek it merge and become one, supplication becomes invocation, the fourth manner of formless prayer. The object of desire now stands revealed as the Infinite. The Quest has begun.

The Prophet, peace and blessings be upon him, said, "Pray as if you see God, and if you do not, know that God sees you." Wherever you find yourself, look for God's signs. Scan the far horizons and plumb the depths of your soul. Contemplate your purity until you are united in spirit with all that is holy. Pursue the one you love behind the fluttering veil of your heart. Imagine him on the Throne at a sublime height. Be continuously conscious that you are in his presence and that he is beholding you. Observe every atom of creation bearing witness to his divinity and perceive that he is both the witnessed and the witness. Abandon yourself in the thought that he is the beginning and the end, the first and the last. Ride the waves of her qualities and plunge into the sea of her existence. Devote your whole being to the search for her beauty, which is so near, yet always just beyond reach. Walk unswervingly, day and night, on the straight path that leads to her. Visualize everything crumbling to dust but her Face.

A pious old man was once performing his ritual prayer under the open sky. A maiden happened to pass his way. Heedless of his ceremony, she sauntered straight across his line of sight. The old man was incensed. He hurried through his remaining prostrations, rose, and called out to her: "Insolent girl, did no one teach you to respect the rite of prayer!" Modestly she answered, "I am sorry, uncle, I did not see you. I am on my way to meet my *bel ami*. My only thought was of him." Hearing this, the old man's rage melted in remorse. This slip of a girl knows the secret of worship, he mused, while I merely go through the motions.

Invocation reaches its perfection in the fifth type of inner prayer, which may be called communion. In communion the worshipper disappears, effaced as stars are effaced when the sun rises at dawn. Daylight shines through windows and walls, flesh and bone, body and mind. The morning bird's trill sounds the note of eternity. Souls rise up from earthen graves and ascend invisible stairs until their blurred forms are lost in light. Rivers spend themselves in oceans, oceans in skies, and skies in the all-pervading life in space. An ancient simplicity engulfs the whole of creation. All is as it always was and ever will be, world without end.

On Alms

*F*ILS *du roi* Gahmuret, everything in the world belongs to the one to whom the world belongs. Nothing is yours or mine. When possessions change hands, nothing really changes. We enter the world empty-handed in the beginning and leave it empty-handed in the end.

No doubt there is pleasure in the finer things of life, in all that is soft to the touch and pleasing to the eye. How well I know the attractions of exotic fruits, lustrous jewels, and sumptuous perfumes. Such dainties do gratify the senses. They mean nothing to the soul, however, unless the Real shines through them. And the Real only appears when the self disappears.

When one looks beyond one's wants one begins to see others' needs. Possessions then seem less desirable. One is less minded to acquire the things of the world and more inclined to give them away. The more one gives the freer one feels. The giver receives as much as the receiver, for the giving of alms is a relief to the soul. Coins are of metal, and metal is the heaviest substance on earth. When great heaps of coins are amassed the soul finds itself buried under them, as under a landslide. It cannot breathe unless the load is lightened.

Having been given so much—having been saved
from the indigence of nonexistence and favored
with the fortune of being, having been fed, clothed,
sheltered, and endowed with blessings and mercies
beyond number—can we possibly imagine that the
great cascade of divine largesse that has so abun-
dantly graced us has its rightful end in the muddy
little puddle that is our self-serving self? Faith in
God is faith in the ceaseless flow of life's abundance,
and almsgiving is the action that follows from that
conviction.

Our blessed ancestor King Sulayman, peace be
upon him, said, "Cast your bread upon the waters."
By this he meant, entrust a part of your sustenance to
the waves of the divine bounty. Trust in the tide that
flows through all that is and will be, for you "cannot
understand the work of God, the maker of all things."

Mutawakkil was a caliph of eminent fame and glory. He had a young slave named Fath whom he doted
upon as a son. One day, swimming in the Tigris, Fath
was swept up in a strong current. Unable to resist the
river's force, he lay on his back and let himself be carried away. When Mutawakkil received the news that
Fath had disappeared, he at once offered a reward of a
thousand dinars to anyone who could find him, dead
or alive. The Caliph swore that he would not eat until
Fath was restored to him.

Seven days later a boatman found the boy in a
hole in the riverbank downstream. Seeing Fath alive,
the joyous Mutawakkil rewarded his rescuer with five
times the promised sum and ordered that half the
wealth of the treasury be distributed among the poor.
He then called for food for Fath, imagining the boy

to be half-starved. Fath, however, assured him that he was well fed, explaining that every day a tray of bread had floated down the river and reached him in his hole. He added that "Muhammad ibn al-Hasan the Shoemaker" was written on all of the loaves.

After some searching, Muhammad ibn al-Hasan was found. When the Caliph inquired why he had sent trays of bread adrift on the river, the shoemaker answered, "I had heard it said, 'Cast your bread upon the waters, for some day it will yield fruit.'" Mutawakkil smiled and ordered that five villages be granted to him.

My son, the ordinance of almsgiving requires that you purify your wealth by giving one-fortieth of what you possess to the needy each year. This much is due. Give it joyfully, without regret, knowing that in doing so you are fulfilling a spiritual imperative.

Beyond the requisite one-fortieth, give freely and often. When your life reaches its conclusion, as my life is reaching its own, you will find that what you truly possess is what you have given. Our Prophet, peace and blessings be upon him, was once presented with a lamb. He divided up the meat and gave it out. In the end, only the neck remained—an unappetizing portion! 'A'isha, God bless her, complained, "Only the neck is left." The Prophet answered, "All of it is left *except* the neck."

In the bazaar sellers tout their wares, customers cavil and haggle, money and goods change hands, and everyone looks out for himself. Business is business. But there is another marketplace, another economy. This is the marketplace of munificence, the economy of the gift. Here, transactions defy the rules of self-interest. Here, a gain may be a loss, and a loss may be a gain.

In giving to another, do not think that you are the giver and the other is the receiver. Think that you are giving God a part of what is due. It is God that gives to the receiver, not you. The Prophet said, "Alms fall into the hand of God, the honored and glorified, before they fall into the hand of the suppliant who receives them."

For a gift to be real it must be freely given; nothing should be expected in return. Where there is an expectation of return, a gift is not a gift but a payment in advance. A payment belongs to the bazaar of the self and its wants; it has no place in the market of the soul and of love.

When you give, give so discreetly that your left hand has no knowledge of what your right hand has given. It is better to withhold generosity than to give with fanfare or to make light of a person whom one has granted a favor. The Prophet said, "When a servant of God performs a good deed in secret, God will inscribe it in secret; if he reveals it, it will be transferred from the register of secret deeds to that of public ones; if he speaks about it, it will be removed from both registers and inscribed in the book of hypocrisy."

It is enough that God, the true giver, knows. Though perhaps even God's left hand does not know what his right hand gives.

On Fasting

FILS du roi Gahmuret, the body is a temple and a miniature of the whole creation. It draws power and pleasure from the minerals, vegetables, and animals it joins to its flesh. The harvest of God's good earth is meant for our enjoyment and for the enjoyment of all creatures. The spheres revolve and seasons turn, frost thaws in the sun, seedpods glide on the breeze, rain soaks the land, herbs grow lush, grains crackle, trees bear fruit, and crystal water bubbles up in springs, all that we may eat and drink. This is Providence, the tireless alacrity of the divine largesse.

You will find, my son, that a modest repast taken with calm mind and contented heart is incomparably more wholesome and satisfying than a lavish feast devoured in wantonness. Let your gratitude keep pace with your appetite. Begin each meal with a blessing and a thought for the less fortunate. Dine alone only when circumstance compels you; bread is best broken with companions. Take less than those who sup at your board and see that they are served first. Partake of nothing of doubtful origin; let your lips touch only what you know to be pure and lawful. End your meal before eating your fill, for a full belly weighs down both body and soul.

Before the coming of our Prophet, peace and blessings be upon him, there were in the cities and deserts of Arabia people known as *hanifs*. Ibrahim, peace be upon him, was a *hanif*, and the *hanifs* of later times were his followers. These men and women were neither Jews nor Christians, though they reverenced Musa and 'Isa, peace be upon them, and studied the Tawra and Injil when chance allowed. The unity of God was the whole of their creed. Their special practice was called *tahannuth*. In the ninth lunar month of the year they would retreat to caves and eyries where they gave themselves over to divine remembrance, abstaining from food and drink from sunrise to sunset. Our Prophet practiced this discipline in a grotto on the Mountain of Light, and was graced with the descent of God's word. The revelations that followed blessed and enjoined the rite of the fast.

The physical aspect of fasting consists in abstention from food, drink, and intimate intercourse. When you cease to eat and drink, the pores of your skin open, noxious residues evaporate, and ether begins to circulate through the body's finer channels. Know, my son, that the invisible template of the body of flesh and bone is a body of light, the soul's subtle vehicle. This luminous body is composed of seven organs of spiritual perception, which pulse in the tailbone, abdomen, heart, right breast, mid-chest, forehead, and crown of the head.

The seven organs are linked together by a web of gossamer threads through which ether ebbs and flows. Intoxicants, whether eaten, drunk, or inhaled as smoke, have the effect of clogging these channels, and even the mild intoxication resulting from ordinary food and drink dulls their activity. When the subtle channels are cleansed, magnetic currents ascend and descend, weaving ever deeper and stronger sympathies between body, mind, heart, and soul.

Forgoing food and drink without complaint, fanfare, or neglect of duty teaches the virtue of fortitude. Better to master hunger than to be mastered by it. Indeed, you will find that the mastery attained in fasting is a formidable force. Once raised up, it stands ready to serve the soul in every domain of life. When this force reaches the fullness of its power, no deprivation will deter you and no temptation will distract you from fulfilling your intended purpose. So long as your soul knows and exercises its sovereignty, your body will remain its faithful man-at-arms.

As restraint on earth is rewarded with enjoyment in heaven, a day's fast is rewarded when it is broken at nightfall. Beware, however, the urge to repay lack with excess. When you break your fast, dine as modestly as you would otherwise dine. Even so, you will notice that your simple fare seems suddenly to possess the rarest and most excellent qualities, as though each date were plucked from the Tuba Tree and each jug filled from the mingled waters of heaven's four streams.

In addition to the essential fast of Ramadan it is well to fast at intervals throughout the year. The first ten days of Dhu'l-Hijjah and Muharram are especially auspicious. In other months, the best days are the first, when the moon is new, the last, when the moon is in darkness, and the middle three, when the moon is full and nights are bright. The best days of the week for fasting are Monday, Thursday, and Friday. So long as you honor the Greater and Lesser Feasts, there is no limit to how often you may fast. You may, if you choose, follow the example of our holy ancestor Da'ud, peace be upon him, and fast every other day. Your princely duties, however, may preclude such austerity.

A further aspect of fasting concerns the tongue. God created the human being as a speaking soul and taught Adam, peace be upon him, the names of all things. Our power of speech is a mirror image of the divine Word. When the mirror is tarnished our words come out garbled, and the music of the spheres is drowned in a cacophony of thoughtlessness.

Our Prophet said: "Five things break the fast: deceit, slander, tale-bearing, perjury, and covetous glances." My dear son, there is no treasure under the sun equal to the value of a man or woman's word. No earthly gain could possibly justify the utterance of an untruth or the breaking of an oath. Your word is the divine light in you; never let it be compromised. Suffer poverty, endure pain, bear every conceivable tribulation, but do not speak a word that you know to be untrue, and having once given your pledge, do not fail to honor it. It matters not in the least to whom a trust has been given—prince or peasant, believer or unbeliever—your word must always be your bond.

Nor could it ever be right to speak against a man in his absence, or still worse, to defame a woman. When gossips prate, as they will, remove yourself bodily, challenge their unworthy insinuations, or keep a solemn and wary silence, but never set the seal of your approval on accusations hurled against one who is not present to contest them. Scandal is anathema to gallant ears.

When her son was soon to be born, an inner voice counseled the mother of 'Isa, peace be upon them both: *Eat and drink, and be at peace. If you see any man, tell him: "I have verily vowed a fast to the All-merciful and cannot speak to any one today."* Silence is a sanctuary. Take refuge in it in time of need. Find relief in silence from the babble of the crowd.

It is rightly said: "The proper answer to a fool is silence." There are times when the whole world seems sunk down in the most wearisome displays of foolishness. Other times one is hard pressed to conceive of a greater fool than oneself. In either instance, silence is a mercy.

A fast is spiritualized when the heart admits no thought or feeling unless it be rooted in the ground of oneness. The heart, given wholly over to the eternal, sees and hears nothing without seeing and hearing the One in it. God Most High has intimated: "The fast is for me, and I am the reward that comes with it." Ibn Gahmuret, this is the reward I wish for you.

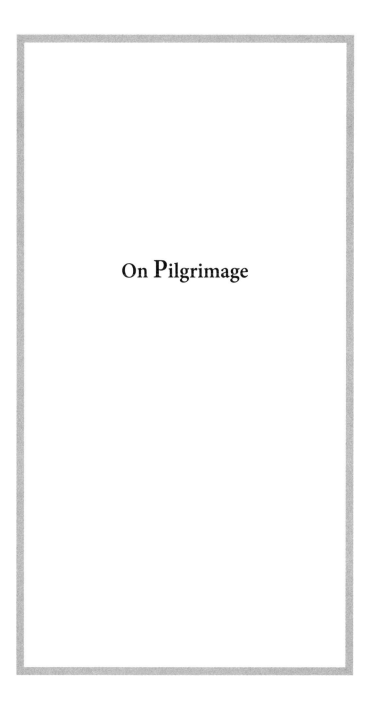

On Pilgrimage

*F*ILS *du roi* Gahmuret, the ways of destiny are inscrutable. Loss follows gain and gain follows loss; what appears propitious in one season proves disastrous in the next; and grace descends when least expected, a merciful bolt from the blue. When Sara cast out Hajar and Ibrahim abandoned her in a sulphurous waste with the infant Isma'il in her arms—peace be upon the four of them—who could have imagined that Providence was working behind the screen, guiding the course of history toward a fuller dispensation of the compassion that is the very taproot and essence of creation?

Desperately Hajar ran between the hills of Safa and Marwa, frantic for water to quench her child's thirst. Isma'il lay in a swoon under a palm, his lips cracked and eyes glazed. At last Hajar stopped to catch her breath. Night had fallen. Overhead the Milky Way shimmered, each star a witness. Whisperings of safety reached her on the perfume of the breeze. She went to Isma'il. Beside him the ground was cool and damp. A spring was welling up.

God does not burden a soul beyond capacity.

The spring was Zamzam and beside it Hajar made a home and raised her son. Once a year Ibrahim would visit, and the time came when he arrived

43

with a mandate from the invisible world. The Holy Indwelling guided him to erect a house to be known as the Ka'ba. And so father and son labored to rebuild Adam's ancient shrine.

In the upper reaches of the higher spheres stands a temple. It is called the Visited House because every day seventy thousand seraphs and cherubs flock to it. Before they enter its enclosure, the angels bathe in a pool of the purest light, mantling their luminous forms in a sheen of glory. Entering, they announce their fealty to the Lord of Hosts, calling out, "At your service!" Then they circumambulate the *sanctum sanctorum* seven times, once for each of the leading names of the Most High: the Living, the Knowing, the Powerful, the Willing, the Hearer, the Seer, and the Speaker. When the rite is complete they fly back to their proper spheres, not to return until the end of time.

My son, the Ka'ba at Mecca stands on earth where the Visited House stands in heaven. The Visited House is the heart of space, and the surging waves of the angelic intelligences are its systole and diastole. The Ka'ba too is a heart. When pilgrims advance toward Mecca they are following a current that flows through all the vessels and veins of the earth.

In the age in which our Prophet was born, Mecca had fallen low and Ibrahim's legacy was all but forgotten among its people. The Ka'ba was crowded with grotesque idols, a gallery of stone wraiths propitiated for ignoble ends. When the Prophet returned triumphant from exile, he swept the house clean.

The Meccans vaguely conceived of a Godhead, whom they called Allah. This entity, however, seemed to them so lofty as to have no bearing on their lives. Better, they thought, to seek the favor of lesser divinities, whose patronage they could buy with appropriate sacrifices and fumigations. Muhammad disabused them of their illusions. All power, he declared, is Allah's. And Allah is near, nearer than we can possibly imagine. No bribes are required for the winning of Allah's favor, for Allah is the very essence of compassion.

At the dawn of time, God offered his Covenant to all of creation. Who would pledge to keep faith with the divine unity in a world of multiplicity? The sky, the earth, and the mountains trembled and demurred. *Man took it on himself.* In the Garden, Adam, peace be upon him, renewed his pledge each year before an angel whom God appointed as witness of the Covenant. But in time Adam forsook his pledge and fell from light into darkness. In his exile Adam landed in Serendib, and God cast the angel after him in the form of a pearl. The pearl seemed a mere stone to Adam until it spoke and revealed its spiritual nature. Overcome with shame, Adam wept and kissed it. As he did so, the pearl became a great black stone. Adam took the stone on his shoulder and carried it to Arabia. There, beneath the Visited House, he established the shrine of the Black Stone, where his descendents might come to renew their pledge.

Ibn Gahmuret, the human heart is the House of the Merciful. The true pilgrimage is the inner journey. The divine presence indwells within you; to find it you must seek it. Sit quietly and close your eyes. Watch your breath. Watch the air enter your nostrils, flow down your windpipe, fill your lungs, and merge into your bloodstream, permeating every limb and organ, from the scalp of your head to the soles of your feet. Then watch the breath leave you, rippling out into the atmosphere, releasing invisible residues. Let your exhalation dissipate until you are utterly empty. For a timeless instant, your existence dissolves. Then the Breath of the Merciful billows, gusts, and pours into you again.

I have shaped him, and breathed my spirit in him.

You are clayed and unclayed with each in-breath and out-breath. When your inhalation reaches its end, pause. Listen within. The heartbeat is faint at first, but it grows in volume as you listen. The listening is not with ears, but with bone and sinew and flesh and blood.

Listen to your heartbeat. Listen to its cadenced throb in your left breast. Feel its reverberation in your hands, feet, neck, and temples. Your whole frame is pulsing. Your body is an ocean heaving with waves beyond count. In the center, your heart is a vortex, endlessly churning.

To reach Mecca from Zazamanc a pilgrim must cross the Red Sea. She will reach her destination if her ship stays above water. The inner pilgrimage is different. To attain the House of the Merciful you must suffer the calamity of shipwreck. Your boat, your worldly self, must be capsized, broken to splinters, and sucked into the whirlpool. You must drink the ocean down to its briny dregs. You must plunge into the abyss and wash up gasping on the other side.

The other side is the Holy House that every pilgrim seeks, be she Sabian, Jew, Christian, or Moslem.

Here all are gathered, and all stand equal before the Lord. Outer distinctions are abolished; the throng is draped in white. Everywhere is heard the cry, "At your service!"

In the House of the Merciful, time slows to a standstill. Past and future are nothing; the present is all. Space rolls up like a scroll. Everything that was, is, and ever shall be—every star and tree and cloud and idea—confesses the evanescence of its form. So confessing, with shattering delicacy it unveils the eternity of its essence. From the first to the last of the centillion and one things, that essence is pure being, the boundless shining forth of the One.

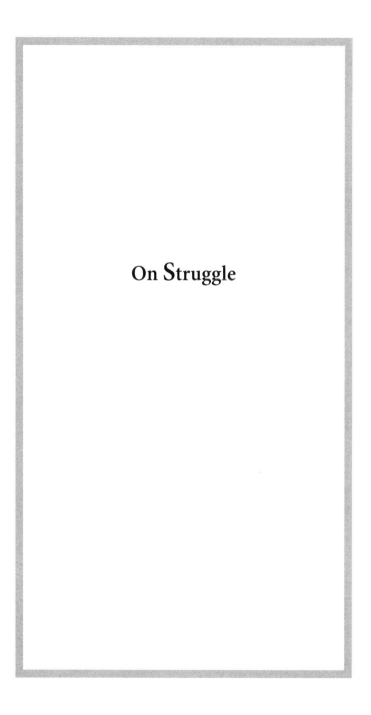

On Struggle

*F*ILS *du roi* Gahmuret, at one moment life is a halcyon idyll and the next a bitter fight for survival. When the movement of the spheres never ceases, when destiny itself is restless, how can a man or woman expect rest? All is in motion. All is in contention. The world is a chessboard on which bodies, minds, and hearts jostle and vie for squares. From strain and struggle both life and death are born.

My son, be strong of body, strong of mind, and strong in the struggle. Do not spare yourself in the work that is yours to accomplish. Fulfill your duty punctiliously. Exert all of your energies. Throw your whole self into the tourney, for the stakes could not be higher.

Islam means submission, but submission is of two kinds: one false and the other real. The false face of submission is weakness, the abandonment of the greatest power the soul possesses, the power of will, the ability to choose. To surrender this power is to become less than human; it is to die spiritually.

The real submission is strength, the full exercise of choice. Strength pursues the good tenaciously, without doubt, fear, complaint, or excuse. Like a candle burning in the night, it shines to the last drop of wax. Strength does not submit because its hand is forced.

It opposes itself absolutely to all coercion. When it submits, it submits only to love.

God does not desire the submission of weak men and feeble women. A drunkard's dizzy collapse is not prostration; it is disgrace. True prostration is a proud act. It is the willful surrender of power before power's perfection.

Some surrender to God in lonely caves and hermitages. Others surrender to her on the battlefield. War is butchery—can it ever be good? Widows and orphans are its yield. Yet there are causes worth fighting for, worth giving up life for.

They say that long ago men and women lived in a state of grace and all was peace and amity. Perhaps such a golden age did once exist, but this much I know: the custom of our day is tyranny and exploitation. Justice is not the natural order of things, not today. If you would have justice, for yourself and for others, you must stand for it and stand ready to die for it.

The duty of struggle is an ordinance of faith. In its pure essence it is a form of worship. In defending the commonweal and safeguarding rights bestowed by heaven, a *ghazi* serves the One. To stand against injustice is to bow down before the Just.

Strive in the way of God with a service worthy of him.

A service worthy of him! That is the Quest. What service shall be required? The worthy knight must be always on duty, always girt in service, spurning indolence and perpetually seeking the next chance to prove the mettle of his devotion to the Real.

My son, defend your sisters and brothers in faith against all tyranny and aggression. Indeed, go further: defend innocent men and women of all faiths, and their holy places. The use of arms is sanctioned in defense of every place of worship. *If God had not restrained some men through some others, monasteries, churches, synagogues, and mosques, where the name of God is honored most, would have been razed.* God's name is honored most of all in the heart that is alive. Do not let a human heart be razed. Killing a human is like killing humanity, and saving one is like saving it.

Animals too possess hearts, and likewise require protection. When the Prophet spied a mother dog and her pups as he led his army to Mecca, he assigned a watchman over them lest they be trampled. On another occasion, when a man took an egg from a nest and the Prophet saw the mother bird flapping her wings anxiously, he ordered that the egg be returned. "Fear God in your treatment of animals," he was wont to warn.

There are circumstances in which compassion compels the use of force. One may be justified in taking the life of an aggressor to save one's own life or that of another—indeed, one may be obligated to do so. Such an act is a grave and solemn one. The slayer's hereafter hangs in the balance. If you must draw your sword, or must command others to do so, be sure in your conscience that you are the defender of peace and not its violator. Take up arms in last resort, when every honorable alternative has been exhausted. *If they are inclined toward peace, make peace with them, and have trust in God.* When you do wage war, assail only combatants. The unarmed are inviolable.

While the spheres turn expect no respite from struggle. Struggle is that for which we were made. Do not, therefore, resign yourself to circumstances or strain against life's needful toil. Resign yourself to struggle, and you will surely meet with peace. *Truly, with hardship comes ease.*

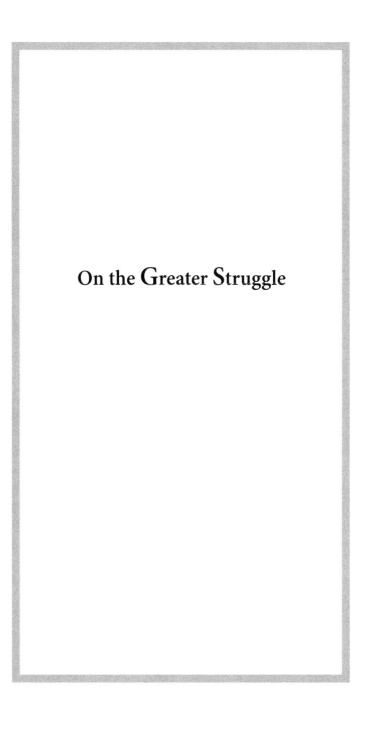

On the Greater Struggle

FILS du roi Gahmuret, it is said that when a contingent of soldiers returned from an expedition, the Prophet, peace and blessings be upon him, welcomed them saying, "You have come for the best, from the smaller struggle to the greater struggle!" Someone asked, "What is the greater struggle?" The Prophet answered, "The servant's struggle against his lust."

My son, there are two domains of life, and the two must not be confused. The first is the world that surrounds you. The world is a battleground where opposites clash, combine, break apart, and collide anew in innumerable rearrangements. You may influence these transformations, but never expect to control them, for they are beyond mortal control. What you can and indeed must control are your own words and actions. These together make up the second domain of life, the ground on which perfect mastery may be realized.

When you have attained self-possession in thought, speech, and deed, you will be free. Yes, the wheel of fortune will keep spinning, and yes, you will be swept up in its revolutions. But fate will not master you, for you will be your own master. No
have the power to alter who you are and w
stand for.

The attainment of mastery requires struggle. The inner struggle is the ultimate struggle, the battle for true freedom. On the battlefield of the soul no effort can be too great and no price too high, for victory there wins peace, and peace is the highest good.

Every human impulse is rooted in the names, attributes and actions of the Sublime Creator. *Say the spirit is of the bidding of my Lord.* Nothing comes from nothing; everything is from him. But in the prism of our narrowness his perfection is curbed and contorted, taking on the aspect of our limitation. We mishandle God's power, and in our clumsy hands it becomes brutality. We neglect the flame of his love, and in our cold hearts it burns down to lust.

When the soul grows negligent the ego revolts, seizes its throne, and exiles it to the Unseen. While the soul floats impotently above, the gloating ego holds court in the body, pressing the soul's once-faithful courtiers into its own nefarious service. Under the usurper's sway the brain becomes a scheming vizier, the eyes prying spies, the tongue a bombastic herald, the hands quarrelsome myrmidons, and the feet a cowardly cavalry. The heart, loyal to the soul to the end, is chained and thrown in the dungeon.

The ego is a chiaroscuro, a portrait in half-light and gloom. Its shade is named the commanding self. *The self commands one to evil, unless my Lord have mercy.* This dark, imperious self is pure appetite. Its sole concern is to indulge its cravings and gratify its conceit at every chance. Enclosed in an impermeable shell of self-regard, it is temperamentally incapable of sympathy and fellow feeling. To the commanding self, others exist only as instruments of its own pleasure, or as threats to that pleasure. It will beseech them obsequiously or harangue them venomously, but it will never take an honest interest in their welfare. Desire is an idea it attaches only to itself. The desires of others are less than nothing to it.

The *blaming self* is the name of the ego's twilit half. Nobler than the commanding self, it is yet too lacking in grace to attain the full stature of nobility. It is its rival's opposite in every respect. While the commanding self disports itself brazenly, the blaming self quivers in shame. Where the commanding self has ambition, the blaming self has hesitation. Its hesitation is not without reason. It fears to cause harm, and herein lies what nobility it possesses. The blaming self is courteous. It considers consequences and recognizes rights beyond its own. It knows that one day it will be held to account.

The commanding self and the blaming self make an awkward pair. One runs hot and the other cold. One lives for the pleasures of this world and the other for the rewards of the next. Never can the two agree. When the commanding self would go north the blaming self must go south. The ego is at a standstill until one or the other prevails.

To every incarnate soul certain requisites are due. A daily loaf of bread, pure water, shelter from the rain, warm clothing, freedom from oppression, and a modicum of dignity are appurtenances without which a human can hardly remain human. When denied, these elementary needs must be forcibly claimed. The Sublime Lord has announced, *We have honored the children of Adam.* Let no man dishonor the one God has honored, and she has honored all people.

The commanding self is within its rights to claim its fair portion. It is necessary that it should, for if it will not defend itself, who will defend it? Its fault lies in overstepping bounds. The commanding self's need has a way of swelling to the proportions of greed. Enough is never enough. The enjoyment of life's simple pleasures does not suffice it. It must possess what its neighbor possesses. It must have what is forbidden. It must sate an appetite so cavernous it can never be sated.

The intervention of the blaming self is felicitous. Boundaries need drawing. All is not permissible. A person's perspective widens when she sees through other eyes. She might in this manner discover that her own good does not and cannot exist at a far remove from the good of her family, the good of her people, and the good of the patch of earth on which she lives out her sublunar days.

The blaming self must be strict and wary if it is to hold in check the frantic passions of the commanding self. The sybarite will send forth its champions: Sir Avarice, Sir Sloth, Sir Gluttony, Sir Fury, Sir Scorn, and Sir Treachery. The penitent must answer with its own redoubtable worthies: Sir Gratitude, Sir Discipline, Sir Moderation, Sir Reason, Sir Courtesy, and Sir Fidelity. To the victor goes the prize, the ego's dominion.

If you would correct your faults, my son, you must in the first place study them. The commanding self boasts of its barbarities or shrewdly conceals them, but it never sees them for what they are: stains and smudges over the glow of the soul. To study the passions, and to direct them to their rightful ends, is the blaming self's calling. Clarity of vision is wanted. Al-Kindi advises a daily practice of accounting. Each evening, he says, one should carry out an examination of the actions of the day. No deed should be overlooked. However small it may be, a fault should not be suffered to slip unnoticed into the cover of night. Shine a light upon it, the philosopher counsels. Stop it in its tracks and reform it, or it will offend again tomorrow.

Mortal as we are, we are fallible, and even the wisest among us never entirely cease to err. Yet the fool and the sage belong to two different tribes. The fool repeats his mistakes endlessly, while the sage's mistakes are always new, always different. When God's perfection is constantly renewed—*every day in new splendor he shines*—why should man's limitation repeat itself?

Al-Kindi urges the disciple of wisdom to learn not only from her own mistakes, but also from the mistakes of others. When we have been sinned against, or have witnessed a sin, we ought not dwell on the thought of the sinner, but rather reflect on how we have been guilty, or might in the future be guilty, of just such a transgression, and how we must strive always to avoid it. Then, instead of provoking our ire, others' misdeeds usefully instruct us on the necessity of controlling our own waywardness.

In its opposition to the excesses of the commanding self, the blaming self is a saving grace, a talisman against the worst kinds of degradation. And yet it too is capable of excess. When its humors are in balance, the blaming self approaches the Sublime Creator with dignified reverence, as a staunch and loyal *ghazi* approaches the Caliph's throne. When distempered, it crouches in fear, conceiving itself the merest of worms, and God an outraged and merciless tyrant. In such a weakened state, it has little power to resist the vices of the commanding self. And so the divided ego swings like a pendulum, lurching between bouts of dissipation and paroxysms of shame, now laughing thunderously, now raining tears.

If the commanding and blaming selves were the only powers on the field, the battle for the ego's dominion might never end. But there is another, a sovereign whose majesty instills awe and deference in the sybarite and penitent alike when she rises to the full height of her glory. I allude to her imperial highness the tranquil self.

A seeker of truth once resolved to draw near to God. He called his ego and said, "O ego, I wish to attain God's presence. Can you help me?" The ego answered, "No, I cannot, for I belong to the world and care only for its pleasures." Dismissing it, the seeker next called his soul. "O soul," he said, "I wish to be with my Lord. Can you help me?" "No," the soul answered, "I cannot, for I belong to the next world, and its celestial delights are my only concern." Losing hope, the seeker summoned his heart. "O heart, I wish for God's nearness," he said. "Neither ego nor soul will help me. Will you?" "Indeed, I will," answered the heart, "for it is he that gave me life when I was dead. I belong to him."

The tranquil self is part and parcel of the mystery of the heart, the throb inside the throb in the human breast. Hovering between earth and heaven, the heart is amphibious—a hybrid of angel and animal, or so it seems. Now it appears sensual, now spiritual, yet it is neither one nor the other, but both, and neither. Its homeland is the place where opposites meet, the place of the presence of the Friend. The Friend is all that it desires, and pain and pleasure are alike to it. It wants only its beloved, and what its beloved wants.

Rabi'a al-'Adawiyya, may God sanctify her secret, once abstained from food, drink, and sleep for seven days, absorbed in constant prayer. Finally, as she was near fainting, someone brought a cup of food. She accepted it and went to fetch a lamp. Returning, she found that a cat had overturned the cup. Resolving to break her fast on water instead, she went to bring a jug. When she returned, the lamp had gone out. As she fumbled with the jug in the darkness it fell and broke. Lamenting bitterly, she heaved such a sigh that it seemed the house might catch fire. She cried out, "O God, what is this by which you are trying me?" A voice answered, "Take notice! If you wish, I will endow you with all of the pleasures of the world, but I will remove concern for me from your heart, for such concern and the pleasures of the world cannot abide together in one heart."

While the commanding self diverts itself with the trifles of the world and the blaming self dreams of the rewards of the next, the tranquil self seeks the face of the Real. Its glance peers through veils, searching behind the patchwork shroud of fragmentary appearances for the deeper contours of the eternal face, the face it lives to adore. Its eyes do not swerve or sweep astray.

When Adam and Hawwa dwelled in the garden, peace be upon them, God the Most High was always before their eyes. Yet they were not dazzled; their hearts were not pierced. Strangers to darkness, they could not know the meaning of light. And so the Creator ordained exile, condemning them to the desolation of banishment that they might one day taste the elation of homecoming. *What is to come is better for you than what has gone before.* From oneness they fell into manyness, from union into separation. They lost the garden of being and found themselves in the jungle of becoming.

Knowledge of the world is the fruit that led man into the jungle and love of God is the fruit that ushers him back into the garden. It was Iblis' duty to proffer the fruit of knowledge and it is the Messenger's task to extend the fruit of love. Love's fruit is like no other. At first it is sweet, then bitter, and finally bittersweet. It is poisonous, but also good medicine. The one who eats of it will suffer the agonies of death, but in time she will rise again more living than before. She will die to herself and rise again in the Real.

Eat the fruit of God's love, my son, and return to his garden. Breathe the weather of the season of the rose. The names of the Most High are seeds. When they quicken in your inner ground, watered by worship and sunned by faith, the garden will spring to life in you. Like a bud, your heart will open, petal by petal, giving forth a ruby light and a heady attar. In your right breast you will then feel a flutter, and—lo!—another blossom, a white flower, more diaphanous than the last, a gossamer bloom of spectral beauty. When you inhale its delicate scent you will know it to be the essence of purity. To the commanding and blaming selves it is a somnolent drug. Let the antagonists sleep, and the tranquil self will awaken. A bud will now open in the middle of your chest. Its light is gold and green. As its petals tear apart, your primal nature will show itself. Summer will arrive in the garden. In your forehead and crown, in your belly and tailbone, in the palms of your hands and the soles of your feet, blossoms will unfurl. Your flesh will become fertile soil, your veins limpid streams. Butterflies will glide on the breeze of your breath.

When all is in bloom, all a riot of color and fragrance, from the tongue of every flower will come these words, and you will know that you have come home:

> *O you tranquil self,*
> *Return to your Lord, well-pleased*
>   *and well-pleasing!*
> *Enter then among my votaries,*
> *Enter then my garden!*

On Chivalry

FILS du roi Gahmuret, it pains me more than I can say that I will not see you grow to manhood. I will not see your form, hear your voice, or feel your touch. Even still, I will turn toward you. Though your face may be veiled to me, I pray and trust that I will be given the sight to see what is in your heart. With eyes of fire I will watch over you, delighting in your happiness and mourning your grief.

Before long you will be a young man. The lengthening of your limbs needs only time; if a boy merely eats, he will grow. But to become a young man in the true meaning of the word, to become a *fata*, a chivalrous youth, something more is wanted. Your nourishment must be virtue. Generosity, courage, courtesy, and wisdom must be your constant practice, Ibn Gahmuret. You must aspire to the knighthood of purity, and you must attain it.

For as long as men and women have risen toward the good in thought, word, and deed, so long has chivalry graced the earth. Whenever revelation has come down, the order of chivalry has rallied to the prophet's call, renewing its fealty to the ancient Covenant. Time and again, with the sweat and blood of its worthies it has redeemed its vow.

The chivalrous youth may be of any age in body, but in spirit she must be young. There is no place in this lionhearted band for the jaded and cynical. And what is youthfulness? Call it unshakable hope, inexhaustible strength. Whether he be young or old, the gallant's lips must always be moist with the water of life. As he sallies out into life's perilous fray, his step should never flag.

The chivalry of men is called *futuwwa*, youngmanliness. The chivalry of women is named *niswan*, womanhood. In the Holy Koran, Ibrahim, Yusuf, Yushua, and the Companions of the Cave are known as *fityan, young men*. Maryam, Mother of 'Isa, is named *nisa*, a *woman*. These are the worthies of the blessed book, patterns for you to live by. Peace be upon them!

The coming of a prophet is a boon to the righteous and a bane to the iniquitous. Ibrahim's birth was foreseen by soothsayers who warned Namrud, the king of Babel, that one was to be born who was destined to topple thrones. The tyrant sent his officers on a mission of extermination, but Ibrahim's mother found refuge in a desert cave, and in that hidden place gave birth to her auspicious child. There she left him, and there he grew to manhood, with reeds for a bed, beasts for playmates, and wild herbs for food.

One night, gazing on the silver beauty of the evening star, the young Ibrahim fell into an ecstasy of adoration. Just then, a cloud parted its veil and the still more dazzling form of the moon stood revealed. All through the night Ibrahim praised the moon's perfection, until at last the moon and stars grew pale. A flame was rising over the eastern horizon. As it mounted higher, it took the shape of a blazing disc of peerless brilliance. With rapt devotion Ibrahim watched the sun's progress across the firmament. Finally it sank down under the western horizon and the sky was again dark. Ibrahim's astrolatry was exhausted.

He closed his eyes. What he saw was not darkness, but light. Celestial bodies might come and go, but this light would remain. It came not from the sky, but from an inner source. Its source was life itself, the kindler of every flame. The Light of Lights would never be extinguished. It was God, the Merciful and Compassionate. And Ibrahim became a *hanif.*

If you close your eyes, Ibn Gahmuret, you will observe a misty glow. Go deep underground, if you will. Close a hundred doors behind you. Shut out the sun with the thickest of walls. Still, you will not see darkness. You have never seen darkness, and you will never see it. Vision is light. Life itself is light. Close your eyes. What do you see? Your mind's eye is awash in fine whirls of color. Let a thought come and suddenly a form takes shape, a luminous figure. When this form fades another will arise to take its place. The inner landscape is as multitudinous as the world without.

Every form is an amalgam of colors. When a form disappears, its colors are not lost; they merely recede, to appear again the next moment in a new admixture. The mind is a palace of mirrors. It contains nothing but colored rays and polished surfaces. The rays career endlessly, braiding an infinite procession of ephemeral forms, all of them woven of the same array of hues. These hues are not substances in themselves. They are, rather, the several refractions of one primeval beam, one pure and eternal light. Nothing exists besides it. All else is reflection, light upon light.

Conceived by light, Ibrahim's faith was soon to be tried by fire. The hand of guidance conducted him from the desert to the city, tasking him to renounce his mystic seclusion and announce the message of God. Some heeded his call, while most persisted in the religion of their fathers, a creed steeped in superstitious ignorance and cringing fear. Among these was the prophet's own father Azar, a seller of idols.

To age and experience respect is due. The cornerstone of a courteous manner is the reverence that is owed to one's mother and father. There are nonetheless occasions, grievous occasions, when obedience to a parent means betrayal of the truth. Faced with such a choice, truth and honor must come first. The imitation of elders is no substitute for true knowledge and right action. Tradition aims to preserve what is wise and good, yet it often bears in its train much that is defective and worthless. Muddled notions gain force by the sanction of hallowed custom. And so, time and again, revelation has come to sweep away the detritus of the past. Hence I counsel you, my son: respect your elders, but make revelation and reason your guides.

When Namrud learned that Ibrahim was in the city proclaiming God's unity, he knew that his fated nemesis had arrived. He tried first to awe him with the rude splendor of his stone pantheon, but when Ibrahim set upon the figures and razed them to the ground, Namrud resolved to rid himself of the agitator once and for all. As a spectacle of his supreme might, the tyrant decreed that Ibrahim should be burned alive in a terrible conflagration. An enormous fire was constructed and Ibrahim was catapulted into its crackling furnace. Inside the fire a wonder ensued. Ibrahim found himself wrapped in the cool embrace of green leaves, fresh flowers, and lush fruits. The blaze that roared around him could not blister his skin or singe his hair. Surrounded by hellfire, he was in a rose bower, a sweet-scented alcove of paradise.

Heaven and hell are not distant realms. Hell's ember-strewn road begins on earth, as does heaven's garden walk. As you travel life's path you will meet inmates of the pit and denizens of the garden. Many more you will meet who have a foot in each place. The people of the fire are loath to burn alone. They will endeavor to spread their fire to you. They will tempt you to join them with enticing allurements. If you refuse, they will pour scorn and wrath upon you until your rage is inflamed. Do not succumb! Do not answer abuse with abuse or you will fall into the pit. Call on Allah, the Uplifter, the Deflector. Remain in the station of tranquility and no harm will come to you. Even an enemy that has gained the power to injure your body cannot touch your mind, your heart, or your soul. Take refuge in the pristine folds of your primordial nature, and so take refuge in the garden.

Say: 'God.' Then leave them alone, playing their game of plunging.

Thanks be to God, if the people of the fire are quick to waylay a lost traveler, the people of the garden are just as quick to help her on. The garden folk turn no one away. They glimpse hope and promise where others see only failure and ruin. They detect a hidden purity where others see only marks of the world's soot and grime. As anger spreads from heart to heart, so does the spirit of peace. The heart that anger and fear has wounded, peace soothes and heals. More eloquent than words is the gaze of the tranquil soul. The knowers know it as the glance of kindness. This glance is a sign, a wordless glimmer of the ancient love that moves the spheres in their courses. Such a sign has been shown down the ages at fateful moments, redeeming and transfiguring the lives it blesses.

Ibrahim survived Namrud's wrath and became a friend of God and a summoner of men and women to the flowerbeds and shade trees of God's intimacy. Abandoning Babel, he took a knight's vow to venture wherever his liege would send him. His companions were his wives: his cousin Sara, and later Hajar. Together they wandered the wastes of Filistin. In Mamre they encamped under an oak tree, pitching tents, unrolling carpets, gathering fruit, and drawing water. Any who approached their oasis was welcomed with a cordial reception. When a stranger appeared, they first hailed him with the salutation, "Peace be upon you!" They next presented him with cool water, ripe dates, and other delicious refreshments. Finally, they opened the doors of conversation, inquiring first of the guest's welfare. Their custom could thus be summed up in three simple but pregnant words: *salam*, salutation; *ta'am*, provision; and *kalam*, discussion.

Bedouins and travelers were wonderstruck at the flood of kindness that overwhelmed them under Ibrahim's oak. They would stammer out expressions of thanks and esteem, but Ibrahim would gently silence them. All bounty is from the Lord, he would say, and all thanks and praises are due to him. Then Ibrahim would invoke God's surpassing glory, his tear-laden eyes uplifted toward the heavens. In this way he delivered the message he was tasked to give, a message that would in time put forth three mighty branches. These we know as the Mosaic, Christian, and Muhammadan religions.

Ibrahim's friendship with God attracted seekers who sought, likewise, to draw near the Friend. Among these, some were by nature solitary and pensive. They thrived under the prophet's tutelage and readily absorbed the mysteries of the inner spheres. Others there were, however, who were cast in a different mold. Their vocation was in the world. Amidst the travails and vicissitudes of mortal fate they strove to enact lives of virtue and devotion. Try as they might, these seekers could not reconcile the saintly path of renunciation with the requirements of worldly duty. They appealed to Ibrahim to open a way for them. The prophet turned within. Before him loomed the heaving, wave-tossed ocean of the mystic quest. He dove into its dark expanse and swam a vast distance. At last an island appeared. It was Sarras, the holy isle of knightly purity. Ibrahim returned to his disciples, fashioned a boat, consecrated it to the divine law, and conducted the gallant amongst them to the blessed isle, that it should be their fortress, and the fortress of their heirs until the end of time. So chivalry was born. And Ibrahim was named its father, Abu'l-Fityan.

From Ibrahim proceed two bloodlines: the lineage of Isma'il and the lineage of Ishaq, may God's peace be upon them both. Through both lines the tradition of chivalry has come down. Among the descendants of Ishaq was Ya'qub, peace be upon him. Ya'qub had many sons, but his favorite was the fair Yusuf, peace be upon him. Yusuf's jealous brothers threw him in a deserted well and left him for dead. He did not die, but was rescued and taken to Egypt, where he lived by turns as a slave, a prisoner, and a minister of state. When his fortune rose, he lavished valuable gifts on his treacherous brothers, saying, *No reproach this day shall be on you; God will forgive you; he is the most merciful of the merciful.* So doing, he showed himself a paragon of chivalry, for as the saintly Abu Bakr al-Warraq has observed, "The chivalrous youth is one who has no enemies."

Yusuf's descendants in Egypt became in time a race of slaves. Their deliverer was Musa, he of the white hand. Musa's companions were Maryam, his sister, Harun, his brother, and Yushua, his page—may the blessings of God be upon them. Yushua was a valiant man-at-arms and a hero of the exodus. When Musa sought the mythic *meeting of the two seas,* Yushua accompanied him. They stopped at a seaside rock, and a salted fish Yushua carried amongst their provisions sprang to life and swam away. Musa did not notice this curiosity, nor in his perplexity did Yushua mention it. After a time they stopped again, and Musa asked for breakfast. Yushua now confessed what had occurred. Elated, Musa declared, *This is what we were seeking!* They returned to the rock, and there found themselves face to face with the Green

Man, the guide of the mystic way—Lord Khizr, peace be upon him.

For his loyal service to the prophet, and for remembering after forgetting, pivoting nimbly on the edge of failure, Yushua is esteemed a chivalrous youth and a model of gallantry.

After Musa came the prophets Da'ud and Sulayman, our holy ancestors. Among their descendants was 'Imran, who married Hanna. To them was born Maryam, the best of women. Hanna's sister Ishba' married the prophet Zakariyya' and bore the prophet Yahya, whom the followers of 'Isa name the Baptist. Peace be upon them!

Maryam was a *woman*, a knightess of purity. She was raised by her mother, and when her mother died, by her aunt Ishba'. When she reached womanhood she took up residence in the temple. Though the provisions of the temple were few, Providence answered all of her needs. A young man named Yusuf came to live at the temple, and the two were joined in virgin wedlock.

One day the angel Jibra'il, peace be upon him, came to Maryam and announced that the Lord had chosen her for a hallowed purpose. Would she receive the divine breath in her womb and become the mother of the Messiah? Maryam gave her fiat and was filled with the word and spirit of God. There is no more eloquent symbol than Maryam of the little soul that faithfully opens itself to the Great Soul, and so receives the seed of a new life, a life that is for the healing of all nations.

When Maryam's womb was quickened she visited her aunt Ishba'. Ishba' was then pregnant with Yahya.

When she saw Maryam the baby within her bowed in adoration and Ishba' was seized with ecstasy. Ishba' related this to Maryam and Maryam answered that, at the same moment, her child had bowed to Ishba's son.

In the depths of every heart, my son, the prophetic presence resides. It is named in scripture *a messenger from themselves*. This inner prophet greets the inner prophet in every heart it meets, though the mind knows it not—unless it be illuminated, like the minds of Ishba' and Maryam.

Maryam was fated to watch her son 'Isa, the Spirit of God, crucified on the hill of al-Juljula. She remained when 'Isa's companions hid themselves. In truth, 'Isa did not die. That which perished was his Nasut, his human nature. The Messiah's divine spirit, his Lahut, lived on and was raised up to heaven. *They did not slay him, neither crucified him, only a likeness of that was shown them. … God raised him up to him; God is all-mighty, all-wise.*

The followers of the Messiah were devoted believers in the unity of the Real. For this the Romans persecuted them mercilessly, taking gruesome pleasure in their death-throes as they succumbed to martyrdom. The emperor Decius was a notorious oppressor of Christians. By his order citizens of the empire were required, on punishment of death, to perform public acts of worship to the idols of the state.

In Ephesus there lived a circle of gallant young Christians. When Decius came to Ephesus he summoned them and bade them choose between their lives and their faith. For these brave souls the choice was no choice; far better to die with faith, they held, than to live in faithlessness. So deciding, they gave away their possessions and retired to a cavern set in the side of a nearby mountain, bringing with them their loyal dog Qitmir. After a time they sank into a deep sleep—so deep that, though days passed, they did not wake. Decius' officers searched in vain. Suspecting the dissenters might be in the cavern, they covered its mouth with stones. In time the youths were forgotten. Years passed. At last, after more than two centuries had elapsed, the Sleepers woke up.

It seemed to them that they had slept only a night. Though they feared capture by Decius's men, they were hungry, and so sent one of their number to buy bread in town. This youth, whose name was Malchus, was surprised to find stones blocking the cave's entry. On removing the stones and making his way to Ephesus, he was still more astonished to see churches where before there were idol-temples. When he tried to pay for his bread with antique coins, the townspeople perceived that a mystery was afoot. They followed him in great numbers to the cave, and there beheld the awakened men. The leader of the Sleepers, Maxmillian, declared, "God has revived us before the Day of Resurrection, that you may believe in the resurrection of the dead." The Companions of the Cave then bowed their heads and their souls flew to heaven.

The Companions fell asleep as reviled outlaws and awoke as sainted heroes! Such are the revolutions of fate. Do not, therefore, submit to the coercion of tyranny, whatever may befall. Better to slumber quietly in the earth, knowing that the day will come when your Maker will awaken you and call you before the only throne that endures, the seat of her eternal love, justice, and mercy.

Ibrahim, Yusuf, Yushua, Maryam, and the Companions of the Cave are the valiant worthies counted as *fityan* and *niswan* in the Holy Koran. If we turn to the sacred traditions of the Prophet another exalted name appears: Lord 'Ali, the Lion of God. For the Prophet said, "the most chivalrous of you is 'Ali." When 'Ali asked the meaning of chivalry, the Prophet answered that it was, "a nobility which ennobles the valorous and generous." He explained that 'Ali's chivalry came from him, and that his own chivalry came from Ibrahim.

Finding himself encircled by attackers at the Battle of Uhud, the Prophet called on 'Ali to drive them back. Despite their number 'Ali held them at bay until, battered to the extreme, his sword shattered. When the Prophet saw this, forthwith he presented 'Ali with his own sword, a relic of the armory of King Da'ud. Proudly uplifting the blessed blade, the name of which was Zu'l-fiqar, 'Ali rushed into the fray and drove back the enemy, though he bled from seven wounds. The Prophet exclaimed, "He is of me and I am of him." To which, hovering above, Jibra'il answered, "I am of both of you." Suddenly, from the Unseen, a stentorious voice thundered, "*La fata illa 'Ali; la sayf illa Zu'l-fiqar*": There is no chivalrous youth but 'Ali, no sword but Zu'l-fiqar!

Hazrat 'Ali's courage was matched only by his generosity. For him, and for his noble wife Fatima the Radiant, may God bless her, to eat when others were hungry was a thing not to be thought of. Once, when their sons Hasan and Husayn were both ill, God bless and keep them, they sought the Prophet's advice. He advised them to undertake a fast, and so they did. On the first day of the fast Fatima baked barley cakes for their evening breakfast, but when 'Ali saw a band of freed prisoners-of-war pass by their home, he gave them the cakes and he and his family went hungry. The next day Fatima again made cakes, but again 'Ali gave them away, this time to a troop of blind beggars. Fatima uttered no word of complaint. Indeed the next day, after baking cakes, she herself gave them to a little throng of underfed orphans. Three days and an evening thus passed and the holy family took no food. In the deep of the night Jibra'il appeared and recited, *Surely the righteous shall drink of a cup whose mixture is camphor, a fountain where drink the votaries of God, making it gush forth plenteously. They fulfill their vows, and fear a day whose evil is on the wing; they give food, for the love of him, to the needy, the orphan, the captive: 'We feed you only for the Face of God; we desire no recompense from you, no thankfulness; for we fear from our Lord a frowning day, inauspicious.'*

Lord 'Ali and Lady Fatima were generous because they knew God to be generous and to love generosity. Their own hunger was to them of little moment. What mattered was that God should smile on them and never frown. Could they look into God's face at the end of time knowing that they had eaten while a helpless sufferer went without food?

Hasan and Husayn drank the spirit of chivalry with their mother's milk, and passed it down to their descendants. 'Ali's disciples likewise transmitted it. 'Ali sent Salman Pak to Ctesiphon, Da'ud al-Misri to Egypt, Suhayb ar-Rumi to Byzantium, and

Abu'l-Mihjan to Yemen—may God be pleased with them. In this way a great wave of illuminated thought, word, and deed swelled and surged through time and across the breadth of the earth.

When corruption and tyranny took hold in the institutions of state, the followers of chivalry's straight path became, like the Companions of the Cave, rebels and dissenters. Their principles were not negotiable, nor could their allegiance be compelled by the powers of the day, for it belonged indelibly to the Power that is forever.

Though chivalry is in essence a sign of the primordial nature of every woman and man, it is also an art of life that grows in depth and subtlety with guidance and practice. Right guidance is necessary for the questing pilgrim. Even Musa the prophet sought guidance, asking it of Khizr.

Squires in the chivalric line receive their training from knight-sheikhs, or knightess-sheikhas, who are living patterns of courage, temperance, wisdom, and justice. The squire must give up all profligacy and frivolity, and pour his energies into the work of sacred reflection and generous action. He must press against the limits of his body, mind, and heart, swimming in frigid waters, keeping vigils in the night, and abjuring every selfish and ignoble impulse that obtrudes on his ideal. The preceptor will watch over him and ensure that strength and grace increase in him in due proportion. As his muscles harden, his heart must in like measure soften and sweeten. The ripening of the heart shows itself in the badge known as the smiling forehead, the bright gleam that shines from the brow of the tranquil.

When the sheikh determines that the squire is ready, he summons him to receive the accolade of knighthood. The orders of Christendom render the accolade by the tap of a sword. We too use the sword, but we also employ the cup and the sash.

The sword is a clear symbol of uprightness, keenness, and brilliance. No weapon is as beautiful, or as dangerous. A naked sword commands attention. The knightess must ever act with the greatest precision and care, and the sword is the sign of her vigilance.

The Refuge of Prophecy possessed seven swords, including Zu'l-Fiqar, which he bestowed on 'Ali. While he lived, the Lion of God kept that holy blade always at his side. When he attained martyrdom Zu'l-fiqar was lifted up to heaven.

My son, when you are of age you shall inherit the sword that your father has left for you. It is a damascened scimitar of the finest temper, as formidable a saber as a *ghazi* could wish. With it, Ibn Gandin saved Zazamanc. God willing, you too shall accomplish feats of surpassing valor.

Eight rules there are that you must observe when your father's sword is yours. First, you must not touch the hilt except when bathed and ritually pure. Second, when taking the sword in hand, you must invoke God's name. Third, when you draw it, you must point it at no one, except in battle. Fourth, having drawn it, you must place it momentarily against your neck, signifying your ego's acceptance of death. Fifth, you must kiss the hilt. Sixth, you must not draw the sword except when necessary. Seventh, when you sheathe it, you must do so reverently. Eighth, you must never leave it uncovered. If a sheath is lacking, cover it with a cloth.

Such is the sanctity of the sword. Alongside it, the instruments of our accolade are the cup of salted milk and the sash. Before the coming of the Prophet, certain men of Mecca practiced a crude chivalry. Their initiation was by the wine cup. When the Prophet revived the chivalry of Ibrahim, he introduced the use of milk. Wine is an intoxicating drink, dulling to the senses, while milk is the nourishing refreshment of the son or daughter of the moment, the child of life's bosom. Hence when Jibra'il offered the Prophet two goblets on the night of his Ascension, one containing wine and the other milk, the Prophet chose the milk, whereupon Jibra'il said approvingly, "You chose nature."

When salt dissolves in milk, its form disappears though its taste remains. So must the self of the chivalrous youth vanish while her soul lives on, imparting its taste, the tang of its life, to the One. Thus did 'Isa describe his disciples as "the salt of the earth."

It happened once in battle that 'Ali's opponent's sword broke and the disarmed fighter pleaded, "O 'Ali, give me your sword." Without pause, 'Ali thrust Zu'l-fiqar into his hands. The man demanded to know why he had so recklessly obliged him, exposing himself to certain death. 'Ali answered that he was sworn to generosity and could not do otherwise. The warrior worshipfully dismounted, professed faith in God's unity, and besought 'Ali to initiate him in the order of chivalry. 'Ali assented, and as no milk was at hand, called for water to be brought and mixed with salt. Henceforth water has been deemed a fitting substitute for milk. What liquid could be more pure? All life springs from water.

The accolade is also given by the tying of a sash. The origin of the sash may be traced to Ibrahim, the father of chivalry. There was a time when Ibrahim enjoyed such wealth and prosperity that the angels were driven to doubt the quality of his faith. Knowing his friend's fidelity to be beyond reproach, God invited Jibra'il to test him. Jibra'il accordingly disguised himself as a Bedouin, climbed a hill, and sang a fervent paean of divine praise. Ibrahim approached him with glowing mien and begged that he repeat his invocation. Jibra'il answered that he would do so for the price of half of Ibrahim's possessions, to which the latter readily agreed. As Jibra'il lifted up his voice, Ibrahim fell in a swoon of rapture. Returning to his senses at last he craved to hear the hymn again, promising to pay all that he owned. When the words had again been chanted, Ibrahim lavished thanks on the Bedouin and led him to his house where he presented him with the sum of his possessions, saying, "For me, God's name is sufficient." Convinced of Ibrahim's sincerity, Jibra'il revealed his identity and bade him keep what belonged to him. But Ibrahim insisted that chivalry demanded that he keep his word. If Jibra'il would not accept his wealth, he would give it to the poor. He then called Isma'il, girded him with a woolen sash, and enjoined him to forever serve the needy. That girding was Isma'il's patrimony, the estate of generosity, benevolence, and worship.

Ibrahim girded Ishaq in like fashion, and Isma'il and Ishaq girded their heirs. Through the ages the hallowed practice continued, so that Ya'qub, Yusuf, Shu'ayb, Musa, Yushua, Da'ud, Sulayman, Ilyas, Zarakiyya, Yahya, and 'Isa—peace be upon them—were all girded, and in turn girded their successors and elect disciples. 'Isa girded Shim'un, who girded Salim, who girded Salum, who girded Sabiq, who girded Khalid, who girded Nawfal, who girded Abu 'Amir, who girded the monk Bahira—may God bless them. In his youth, the Prophet traveled to Syria with his uncle Abu Talib. In the course of the journey they chanced to encounter Bahira. The anchorite at once perceived the signs of prophecy in the young Muhammad and presented him with the blessed sash that was his heritage from the Messiah and, now, his grateful legacy to the Messenger.

Near the end of his earthly life, at the pond of Khumm, the Prophet announced to his assembled Companions, "For whomever I was his master, 'Ali is his master." He then called 'Ali to his tent, performed a prayer, and bound a sash around 'Ali's waist. He tied it with three knots, signifying the realities of God, the Angel of Revelation, and the Messenger.

These, my son, are the origins of Saracen chivalry. Your father's sword will be yours. I have inscribed these pages that you may learn the just and proper use of it. Follow my counsels, enter the discipline of a sanctioned and illuminated sheikh, practice wisdom, courage, temperance, and liberality, and one day, God willing, you will attain the dignity of a knight of purity.

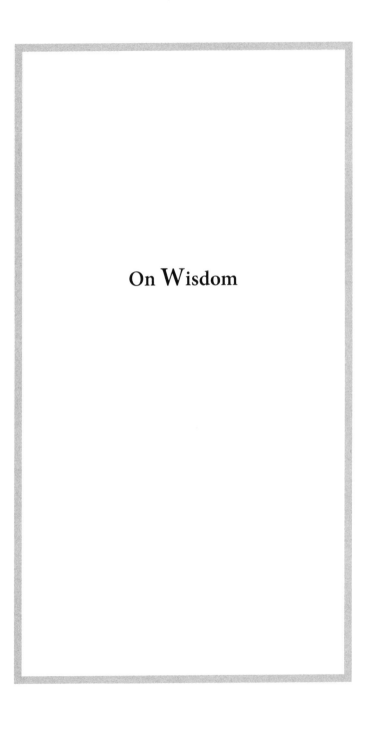

On Wisdom

FILS du roi Gahmuret, the bounteous Lord, may he be glorified and exalted, said through the blessed lips of the Messenger: *I was a hidden treasure and I longed to be known, so I created the world that I might be known.* Consider these words carefully. God was once a veiled mystery, known to no one. Earth was a formless void, and God was alone, wrapped in the impenetrable night of oblivion.

Hold your breath. For a moment you will taste a small gulp of timelessness. But then pressure begins to mount. You need to exhale, to release the spent air in your lungs. The need you feel is a pale and distant echo of the primal necessity that occasioned the world. The Names of the Real were pent up, straitened in the dark confinement of unknowing. So much haunting beauty was there, so much to exalt and adore, yet no daylight, and no eyes to see.

A wave of yearning upwelled in the stillness of eternity. As it crested, the One heaved a sigh of merciful ardor. On the current of that warm suspiration the Names billowed into being. When at last the sigh cooled, its form was a cloud swirling with infinite possibilities. In its writhing vapors were prefigured every face and form destined someday to bear the weight of matter. By and by the chaos of that phantom cloud gave way to the emergence of order, and from its substance was born the glistering expanse of the starry sky. Stars and planets hurled through space, as now they hurl and spin, moved by the inexorable passion of the Creator.

Every fragment and fiber of creation exists to celebrate the glory of the sacred mystery that stands openly revealed in the panorama of the heavens and the earth. The world is the theatre of the divine revelation, and within this bewildering spectacle you and I, and indeed everyone and all things, are at once spectators and performers, witnesses of the perfection of the Real and embodiments of that perfection, however imperfect we may be.

Our purpose is to know and worship God to the fullest of our powers. And how may we know God? The Messenger said, "Who knows himself knows his Lord." Know what is within you and you will know all there is to know.

The human form was fashioned in replica of the divine image, every contour conforming to symmetries as old as time and space. The body contains the constellations, the planets, the sun, the moon, and all that belongs to the earth. The world is a tree and the body is its seed. In the seed the whole tree is encapsulated.

Study nature in the horizons and in yourself. Observe the continuities between your body and the land, and between the land and its source. The stones, rivers and birds, and we together with them, partake of an ancient oneness, a silent communion that weaves its invisible weft through all things.

Dhu'n-Nun the Egyptian alluded to this enchantment when he said, "O Lord, whenever I heed the voices of the beasts, the rustle of the trees, the purl of the waters, the songs of the birds, the delight of the shade, the roar of the wind, or the rumble of thunder, I find in them testimony to your unity."

Four ancient presences surround and pervade us through the length of our lives. These primeval powers live and breathe and even think and speak after a fashion, though their language is so murmurous and arcane few can comprehend it. I speak, of course, of the elements: earth, water, fire, and air. These are the Lord's terrestrial servants and witnesses of being.

Earth is the heaviest of the four, and so the lowermost, the deepest in humility and surrender. Earth is always underfoot. Watch your step! Walk on the ground as you would tread on the skin of a gargantuan beast, for the landscape is alive. Sense the soil and stone beneath you with each footstep. See how the earth pulls you, how it tugs at your bones. But for that pull you would be lost in space. Earth holds you, as she holds the moon, delicately in her embrace. Gravity, as the good doctor Ibn Sina explains, is a species of *'ishq*, of passionate attraction.

In the winter the land is stark and barren, the trees bereft of leaves. Life is hidden underground, occulted in roots and seeds and the secret wealth of untold minerals. Then spring comes, and with it rain. Suddenly the wilderness is carpeted with greenery and festooned with flowers. *You behold the earth blackened, then, when we send down water upon it, it quivers, and swells, and puts forth herbs of every joyous kind.*

How many men and women have lived out their days painstakingly feeding, bathing, and guarding their bodies, meticulously directing the smallest gestures of their limbs and digits, only, in the end, to surrender their shape and form to the ground, to be effaced and—save in the memory of the Omniscient—forgotten? How many bodies lie entombed in the earth; how many silhouettes—of men and beasts and flowers that once momentarily bloomed—now sleep underground?

When you read this, my son, my own form shall be among them.

As many as have perished and turned to dust, so many shall rise from the dust and take form. Innumerable faces of bewitching beauty await their day in the sun. The earth is restless, ever churning, ever quickened anew by the touch of the Living, the Eternal. The substance of your body is not your own. It belongs to the land. All that ever has flourished and perished is mingled in the matter of your body, and so shall your body be mingled in the fabric of the forms ordained to come and go in continuous procession until the end of time, when all forms shall be at once recalled to life and brought before their Fashioner.

Water is an unambiguous sign of the mercy of the Merciful. To dry lips and wilted leaves the moist touch of water is the very kiss of life. That kiss is rendered alike to the rich and the poor, the sinner and the saint. Yet to one who thirsts, a cup of water is the most precious of things. A parched king would readily trade his kingdom for it.

From water a man or woman may learn tact and finesse. Water is never brutish or obdurate. It glides fluidly around obstacles with a cheery splish-splash, wending its graceful course toward the wide ocean of its liquid dreams.

Fire is the heat and light without which the world would freeze in darkness. The green leaves of plants unfurl toward the sun and drink the fire of its radiance. When we eat these plants, or the flesh of animals that have eaten them, we devour fire. Our bodies are perpetually burning, constantly glimmering and glowing. Iraqalitus likens the soul to a flame. When it leaves a body, the body goes cold.

Fire is ardor. Let your life purpose be kindled and the blaze of that master passion will consume the whole matter of your mind and heart, casting its brilliance on the path before you and reducing to cinders every lesser desire. Quoth a sage, "Love is a fire; when it befalls the heart, it burns away all but the well-beloved."

Air is the subtlest of the elements; so subtle, it eludes sight. Yet we feel its touch on our cheek and its flutter in our hair. To breathe is to drink the air, to fill one's frame with it. A breeze swoops down from the sky, sweeps into your nostrils, slides down your windpipe, puffs out your lungs, and spills into your blood, so that it quenches the thirst for breath in every fiber of your flesh.

See the freedom that air enjoys! Nothing can hold it down or fix it to a form. It knows the peace of the upper altitudes, where heavy woes are a thing unknown. Clear, light, and simple, it blows where spirit sends it and asks no questions.

If you would befriend the elements, greet them each morning after rising. Stand before an open window, or outside. Turn your entire attention to your breath. Breathe in through the nose and out through the nose five times. This is the breath of earth. The direction of its current is horizontal, like the ground spread out before you. Its color—yes, as your inner eye opens you will find that even breath has color— is ochre. Feel the bones in your body; these are the stones in you. Sense your flesh; this is your loam. Hear the rumbling call addressed to your skeleton by the granite and sandstone in the ground, and the answer your skull and bones intone. The qualities of earth will show themselves to you, God willing, and you will touch the virtues of patience, endurance, and humility.

Next breathe in through the nose and out through the mouth five times. This is the breath of water. Its direction is downward, as water flows. Its color is green, the color of the sea, the oasis, and the genius of water himself, Lord Khizr. Feel the pulsing flood of blood and lymph surging through your arteries and veins. See how the waves in your veins are of a piece with the storming, gushing, frothing deluge that tumbles across continents and seeps into all things. Witness the unbounded generosity of water.

Now breathe in through your mouth and out through your nose five times. This is the breath of fire. The direction of its current is upward, the direction of a flame's flicker. The color of the fire breath is red, the red of burning coals and tongues of fire. Feel the heat of your body, how it warms your flesh and sends its radiance into the surrounding space. The sun's light warms all that it touches. The whole of the earth, and all who walk upon her, are bathed in the sun's glow, warmed to the marrow of our bones. Fire is vision in the mind and ardor in the heart.

Finally breathe in through your mouth and out through your mouth five times. This is the air breath. The current of air is zigzag, moving inscrutably this way and that. Its color is the blue of the sky, the azure of sublime immensity. Feel the sky engulf your body, rendering it insubstantial—pure breath. Give yourself over to the exaltation of freedom from every earthbound encumbrance.

When you have finished, return to your natural respiration, sensing the presences of earth, water, fire, and air balanced within you. As its architecture now clearly reveals, your body is a temple. Consecrate this earthly sanctuary to the bounteous Lord, and ask for his ceaseless compassion, protection, and direction.

As the sublunary elements dwell in you, so too do the celestial lights that circle above. Chief among these lights are the sun and the moon. In the day we work and in the night we sleep. The sun irradiates our labor while the moon illuminates our slumber. One disc follows the other and both appear to our eyes exactly the same size. The light of the sun is warm and vigorous. The moon's light is cool and languorous. *It is he who made the sun a radiance, and the moon a light.*

Watch the sun as it rises, casting its brilliance across the land and illuminating the whole of creation. The solar disc soon becomes too bright for mortal eyes to bear. If you would take in its rays you must gaze on their reflection on the surface of a pool, stream, or bowl of water. Flashing from the water's mirror, the light of the sun will pierce your eyes and light up your brain. Your thought and emotion will become luminous, and a dazzling fountain will rise up through your crown, plash down over your trunk and limbs, and enrobe you in a mantle of radiance.

The moon may be looked on without intermediary. Moonlight is cool and diaphanous, its beams like the dewy threads of a spider's web. It is a worthy practice to greet the new moon when it first appears each month. When the moon is full, and you are free, go up on the roof and lie under its light. Let its rays wash over you, purifying you of all murk and gloom.

The sun's radiance partakes of the Creator's *jalal*, or power. It is active, positive, and forceful. Its current flows through your right nostril. When you would accomplish something, this is the force you must draw upon. The moon's light, in turn, is of the nature of the Creator's *jamal*, or beauty. It is passive, negative, and receptive. Its current works through your left nostril. When comprehension is needed, and when intuition is sought, this is the quality of breath you require.

In the spiritual bodies above and the material bodies below, in the stars and elements and minerals and plants and animals of this sphere we walk—aye, wherever you look—God's signs are manifest in dizzying profusion. All of nature is providential grace and immortal love. Your body is a microcosm of the whole, a noble mirror held up to the measureless totality. So too is your mind, if you would peer into its depths.

The path of wisdom is the art and science of the mind. Its winding course leads from self to selflessness, and back to self again. Yes, the path is circular, but in the end something is gained—or should I say something is lost? Either way, it is a path we were created to travel. Life is a road, and as the saying goes, the road is no place to settle down.

The science of mind begins with concentration. Little can be expected of a mind that is constantly flitting from thought to thought. Such a mind is the servant of its thought stream, never its master. Mastery requires calm and focused attention. Silence is crucial. With practice, silence becomes deep and still. Set aside a period for silence each day. Indeed, do more: practice long stretches of silence whenever duty permits. Practice forty days of silence and you will hear the world with new ears.

Just as you must silence the tongue, so must you silence the body. Silencing the body means practicing stillness. Learn to sit still without the slightest movement. Shibli, may God sanctify his secret, learned the art of contemplation from a cat watching a mouse hole. Not one hair on its body moved. Sit still and watch your breath with feline vigilance.

As your limbs relax and your breath slows and deepens, your mind will become supple and malleable. You may now profitably practice the discipline of concentration. Begin with open-eyed concentration. Place before you a stone or flower. Stones reflect the *jalal* force, flowers the *jamal* force. Sit motionless and observe the object. Let everything else fade into insignificance, so that there is nothing in the world but your gaze and the object it rests upon. Let the object enter you and fill your mind. If your attention should wander, bring it back at once to the object. Do not muse over the object; simply witness it, take it into your mind exactly as it is. Gradually increase the duration of your practice every day, so that in time you are able to witness the object with unfaltering attention for a goodly period.

The next step is to concentrate with the eyes closed. After gazing on an object for a spell, close your eyes and retain the image. It is important that the entire image be preserved. If the image begins to fade and you cannot accurately recall it, open your eyes, receive it again, and continue. Each day, slightly lengthen the duration of the exercise.

A further step is to visualize an object and maintain it in your mind's eye with steady focus. If you would have inspiration, choose a heavenly shape, a star or crescent moon. If you would have attainment, picture an earthly shape, a flower or stone.

When you have attained proficiency in concentration you will be prepared to practice contemplation. In concentration one is concerned with an image; in contemplation one deals with an idea. An idea is more subtle than an image; it belongs to a higher plane of thought. Nonetheless, it requires the same rigor of attention.

The most elevating themes for contemplation are the names of God, the qualities of the Real. The Prophet said, "Qualify yourself with the qualities of Allah." How could one otherwise make progress on reality's path?

Life has its felicities, but also its adversities. One is wont to welcome the one and bemoan the other. Yet in the great scheme of things, hardship is as providential as ease. Virtue that is not tried and found true is no virtue at all. The blows of fate reveal the lineaments of a man or woman's character. Annoyances and provocations are not what they seem. Life's tests are summonses from on high.

However the wind may howl and rage, keep your footing. Resentment and self-pity are the most futile of sentiments. Rise to every challenge with a smiling forehead and a faithful heart. Mere reaction is unworthy. Let every act of your tongue and hand bespeak the ephemerality of mortal life and the eternity of God.

Sometimes the straight path is difficult to discern. Entanglements snare you and the course of duty is not clear. At such moments your prayer must be, *Ya Rabb fahhim li, ya Hu*: O Lord, give me to understand, you who are the essence. The answer, when it comes, will be a sign disclosing what is asked of you. You will be shown the name among God's names that you must invoke and serve with the whole of your body, heart, and soul.

Make this name your shield and sword. Recite it by tongue a hundred times each morning, and by heart all through the day. Immerse yourself in its sound and sense, so that its influence seeps into the marrow of your bones.

Each name is a profound expanse. The deeper you dive the more will be revealed to you. You will come face to face with the inner textures and gestures of the name, its shades and tones and ethereal rhythms. In your rapture you will begin to comprehend—if such a mystery may ever be comprehended—the wondrous love and hope that moved the Creator to the act of creation and the utterance of the fateful word, *Be!* The world must be that the names may take shape and form and fulfill their ancient promise in ever-new geometries of meaning. Your existence is for no other purpose. If you call upon them, and do all that is within your power to serve them, the names will thrive in you. Your glance will become a corridor between heaven and earth.

Such is the contemplation of the most beautiful names. Contemplation leads, at last, to meditation. In meditation the qualities of being dissolve in the essence of being, the fathomless reality of the Godhead.

There are those on whom the state of meditation descends effortlessly. They are known as the compelled. Those who seek out the Real are called wayfarers. The method of wayfarers is to rise from earth to the highest heaven world by world.

The first plane is called Nasut. This is the material world, the sphere of the senses. Begin here. Close your eyes, relax, and let your breath slow and deepen. Turn your full attention to the surface of your skin. Feel your feet on the ground, the clothes draped over your trunk and limbs, and the gentle touch of the air on your face, neck, and hands. Breathe in this awareness. Now turn your attention to the water of your mouth. Drink its savor. After a time, consider the fragrance of the air you breathe. Investigate its bouquet, its mélange of scents. Then prick up your ears and absorb the medley of sounds that clang, hum, and whisper around you. For a moment, live in a world of vibration. Now, keeping your eyes closed, gaze through the screen of your eyelids and examine the brilliance that meets your glance. Finally, take up all five senses at once, feeling, tasting, smelling, hearing, and seeing all that communicates its presence to your earthly body. This totality is Nasut.

The next plane is Malakut, the world of mind. The objects of your five senses are not the only contents of your awareness. Images float through your psyche: pictures from the past, faces of absent friends and acquaintances, desiderata, faery forms. To rise to Malakut you must now cease to attend to your senses, and give yourself wholly over to the wanderlust of your fancy. Dream as you dream in the night, only keep awake. In this dreamscape are the reflections of all existing forms, as well as the eidola of forms as yet discarnate. They hang suspended as images are suspended in a mirror, only here there is no metal substratum, indeed no substratum of any kind. The images float and whirl in the void. The whole world is here, spinning in ether, disburdened of matter and elevated to the brink of incorporeality.

Beyond Malakut is Jabarut, the plane of pure light. When your arc of thought rises above both sensation and imagination you will find yourself here. At the upper reaches of Malakut forms blur and decompose, melting into throbbing pulses and flashes of light. Seraphs and cherubs soar here in prodigious flocks, each one a lancing ray from the golden effulgence of the Holy Spirit. Enter Malakut and you will enter the inner life of the stars. You will discover a universe of light without time, place, or substance. On earth, light reveals its object to another. In heaven, light reveals itself to itself. The light that will appear to you in Jabarut is the luminous presence of your own soul.

To rise higher than Jabarut is to reach the aurora of creation. Here, in pristine grandeur, loom the archetypes on which every denizen of manifestation is modeled. These are the ancient sources of destiny, the primal impulses and sovereign passions that preside over the course of becoming. You have reached Lahut, the seedbed of the garden of creation. The contours of God's Face have been unveiled to your eyes. You may no longer reckon your body, heart, or soul as your own. It is his Life that lives in you.

Past Lahut you may not go. Beyond lies Hahut, where there is room only for one. Here is a purity beyond all imagining, for here dwells the one Being, free of all accretions, alone in the stillness of eternal solitude. To reach the threshold of this court is to attain the pinnacle of meditation.

And what comes after meditation? In a word, realization. The knowers say that the journey to God has an end, but the journey in God is endless. Realization is the journey in the Real. It is to walk on earth while your gaze is in heaven and your heart betwixt and between. It is seeing God's face glimmering behind every mask, and deeming your own face the flimsiest of disguises. In this manner you will become as a fish in a shoreless ocean of light—a fish through whose little eyes the ocean tours its own depths.

On Courage

FILS du roi Gahmuret, a man's courage is the measure of his faith in the Real. Faith begins in belief. And what is belief? It is of two kinds, the belief of custom and the belief of tradition. Customary belief is a crude species of conviction. As the father thinks, so thinks the son, indolently preferring to inherit his sire's opinions than to form his own well-considered judgments.

In penning these counsels, my aim is not to press you to assume the burden of my notions and attitudes. My experience of life was mine, and yours shall be your own. Just as I possess a knowledge that is unique to me, you shall come to possess your own unique knowledge, your own angle of vision. I write these words only that you may build on my foundation. Put my admonitions to the test, and when in doubt as to their suitability, follow your own lights. By this I mean, act always on your own highest intuition of the truth.

The nobler kind of belief consists of confidence in what has come from sacred tradition: the divine speech embodied in scripture, the hallowed acts of the prophets, and the methods and manners of the saints and masters who followed after them. In these sources rests a higher guidance. Yet even here problems arise. The first difficulty is that words and deeds of the past are often misremembered, so that what was truly said and done is forgotten, while what was not said or done is remembered. The second difficulty is that even that which is rightly remembered belongs, in its particularities, to its own time and place. Revelation does not descend in a void. Revealed guidance responds at urgent moments to tangible needs. Since needs change as circumstances change, the guidance of the past must be interpreted anew in every era.

Such are the two kinds of belief, and such are their limitations. When belief matures it grows into faith. Belief is an egg and faith is the birdling that bursts through its shell and, when its wings are grown, leaps from its nest. At first the fledgling falters and plunges earthward, but at the last moment, when catastrophe seems certain, an ancient instinct asserts itself. The fledgling spreads its pinions, beats the air with firm strokes, and begins to rise. As it gains confidence, it rises higher, soaring at last into the cerulean heights. It has learned trust in the mystic affinity of feather and breeze.

When we say *subhana'Llah*, praise be to God, we use a word which means, in its root, to swim or float. To glorify God is to swim in the heavens like a bird. *Do you not see the birds held high between the heavens and the earth? Nothing holds them but God.*

Your heart will learn to fly when it comes to rely on the Real as a bird relies on the air. The essence of the Real is hidden, yet creation would crumble to dust if the sustaining grace of the Real should withdraw. Here and in the hereafter we are wholly sustained by divine love, a sustenance that knows no limits.

Reliance on God is not complacency. The divine action that sustains us does not merely work upon us, bestowing material favors, but also works in us, directing the instrument of our will when that instrument is rightly tuned. To have faith is to act on the heavenly guidance revealed within you, however exacting its demands.

Nor is reliance on God wishful thinking. Destiny is inscrutable, and a sweet expectation frequently proves the prelude to a bitter disappointment. No, reliance is not expectation. It is, rather, trusting that the Real will be with you wherever you find yourself. In gain and in loss, in pleasure and in pain, in company and in solitude, here and in the hereafter, the most perfect of presences will always accompany you. You will never be alone, never lost to God's love. *He is with you wherever you are.*

The one whose faith is yet unborn lives in dread of the specter of eternal night. In his unease he clings anxiously to what pleasures and privileges he can amass, little fathoming the secrets of his soul's destiny. Sacrifice is to him unthinkable, since any diminution in his standing and holdings seems a step toward death, and the cold of the tomb is what he fears most.

Faith in the Real gives a woman the strength of a lioness. She may in modest measure enjoy the pleasures of the world, leastways the simplest and purest of them, but she is not a pleasure seeker, nor does she want fame. She lives for the One. No one can take anything from her, for in her heart she possesses naught but her dedication to her well-beloved, and no force can alienate that singular devotion from her breast.

Courage is shown in the willingness to sacrifice. The dearer the pleasure or privilege sacrificed, and the higher the purpose for which it is sacrificed, the more noteworthy the deed in the discerning eyes of the angels who are the scribes of earth's hidden history.

Sacrifice sometimes takes the form of the renunciation of a sum of wealth, or of the prospect of material gain. Other times it is status that must be abandoned. To relinquish a life station that favors its bearer with power, prestige, and security asks a fine caliber of courage. For one whose courage is perfected in faith there is no advantage too precious to forego for the sake of a worthy ideal. The possessor of indomitable courage is prepared to lay down even her life for the true, the good, and the beautiful.

Courage is not recklessness. There is in it no streak of swaggering bravado, nor any hint of gloomy despair. One might call it the golden mean between hope and fear. Where there is dignified regret for an imminent loss or apprehension of danger, coupled with an unshakeable resolve to endure the loss or peril for a higher purpose, without a word of complaint—there is courage.

In one fashion or another, change must be countenanced. The vicissitudes of fate may be confronted with confidence or suffered with fear, but they may not long be deferred. All that is built of matter will one day crumble, and all who are born of flesh and blood will one day die. Every change is a little death and a little birth. At last will come death itself, and resurrection. Knowing that death is certain, the choice before every man and woman is to greet it with grace or to grasp hopelessly at the sifting sands of time.

The prophets and friends of God are models of courage in the face of death. Consider 'Isa, who ventured to Jerusalem though he knew the peril. In the garden of Ghatsamani he awaited arrest. He bid his disciples to stay awake with him, but one by one they succumbed to sleep. Foreseeing the torture and execution that lay ahead, he prayed with mingled sorrow and faith, "If this cup may not pass away from me, except I drink it, your will be done!" So hot was the Messiah's sweat—he who had healed the sick and raised the dead—that it seemed his very lifeblood oozed from the pores of his skin.

Consider the leave-taking of our Prophet, the Messenger of God. As his life drew to its close, he led a final congregational prayer, asking for forgiveness for those who had opposed him. When he retired, the Angel of Death approached him with deference and begged to know his wishes, whereupon the Messenger instructed him to conduct his soul to its Maker. He presently whispered words in Fatima's ear that caused her to cry, and then whispered other words that made her smile. She later explained that he said first, "I shall die today," and then added, "I have prayed to God to reunite you with me, as first of my house, and to place you beside me." The Messenger lay on 'A'isha's bosom, sweat pouring from his body. In a swoon he uttered, "The Highest Friend!" He then exclaimed, "Prayer! Prayer! You shall hold together so long as you pray together. Prayer! Prayer!" These were his last words.

Hazrat 'Ali's death was likewise a picture of dignity and good cheer. He had just awoken and was stepping out to perform his morning prayer when the assassin Ibn Muljam emerged from the shadows and struck him down. In the throes of his agony, 'Ali joyfully exclaimed, "I am victorious, by the Lord of the Ka'ba!" Death was to him the promise of new life. *Do not say of those slain in God's way, 'They are dead'; rather they are living, but you are not aware.* As he lay dying he counseled his sons, then said no more except to repeat *no god but God* until his final breath.

Hazrat 'Ali's eldest son Imam Hasan was poisoned by an intriguer. As he lay in extremis his brother Husayn—may God bless them both—begged of him the name of the perpetrator, that he might exact justice. Hasan refused, insisting that to bear tales was a violation of the chivalric code. If he were to divulge the name, he said, he would be unable to face his father on the Day of the Gathering. Musing on the approach of death, he said, "O my brother! I am to attain something the likes of which I have never attained."

Imam Husayn became a martyr soon after his brother. The people of Kufa called him from Mecca to lead them, but as he and his family drew near, the governor's army surrounded the party on the plain of Karbala. Appeals to justice and honor fell on deaf ears; Husayn and his kin were granted leave neither to return to Mecca nor even to draw water from the Euphrates to quench their burning thirst. At last, on the tenth of Muharram, the governor's forces attacked and the Imam's valiant party was massacred. Husayn suffered thirty-three stab wounds and thirty-four blows. When horses had been made to trample his noble body, his head was cut off and mounted on a spear to be presented to the Caliph Yazid.

Among Husayn's foes, one proved himself a man of honor. His name was Hurr ibn Yazid. When he saw the justice of Husayn's cause and the injustice of his masters, he brooded and said, "By God, I am making a choice between hell and heaven." Steeling himself, he changed sides to join Husayn's defenders, hopelessly outnumbered though they were. His blood soaked the sand of Karbala, but his soul rose to the fragrant parterres of paradise, or so must we believe.

On Temperance

*F*ILS *du roi* Gahmuret, the way to the eternal goal is the *straight path*, the middle road that wends its course between all unhappy extremes. Having come from the pure source, we are en route to the pure goal. The soul is a ray of heaven. Let your sayings and doings speak of your kinship with Aldebaran, Benetnash, Rigel, Vega, and the whole starry brotherhood of the night sky. Do not give in to dark whisperings. Stand on your dignity and hold to your principles. Dishonor is the worst poverty.

Never disregard shame, my son, for it is a trusty guide on the straight path. When the croak of fear or the siren song of lust lures you off course, it is shame, ever vigilant, that will call you back. To command your attention shame will stab your heart and make the blood sing in your ears. Do not begrudge shame's heavy hand, for you might not have otherwise listened.

Without shame there is no honor, without honor no dignity, and without dignity the soul is a guttering flame in the wind.

Hold yourself to the highest of standards and expect of yourself the purest correctness. From the world, however, expect nothing. Indeed, stand prepared for anything.

Surprise is the sign of deficient wisdom. All is possible, and every possibility will one day be realized. Circumstances cannot remain as they are. Every day, indeed every moment, brings alteration. There is no standing still and no going back. The whole teeming mass of creation is on the march toward an unseen horizon, and not an atom is suffered to lag behind.

Do not curse fate. Bow, rather, to the cause behind all causes. Extend a courteous welcome to the rising tide of reality's ocean. What arises is what is meant to be. The author of all that transpires is God.

This is not to counsel complacency! Though what arises is what is meant to be, it may not be meant for long. Indeed, it may be your destined duty to oppose, to challenge, and to overturn a good number of the circumstances and forces you are fated to encounter in the course of your life. For your actions and aspirations too belong to the inexorable workings of God's decree.

Indeed, the highest degree of divine will may be found in the perfection of human nature. God has given us freedom, and within that gift rests the sweetest good and the vilest evil. The angels questioned God's gamble, asking, *Will you place one there who would create disorder and shed blood, while we intone your litanies and sanctify your name?* The Lord's answer was to the point: *I know what you do not know.*

God knew that the angels were right, that our freedom opened the world to evil, and to the sorrow that is evil's harvest. But he knew more. He knew that this freedom the angels so dreaded prepared the ground for a good the likes of which they could never dream. That good is the love and devotion that is freely chosen.

The seraphs and cherubs worship because it is their nature, their instinctive share in the order of things. When man worships, loves, and serves, it is because he has resolutely found his way to the throbbing heart of being. Love that is enforced is not yet true love. Love in its perfection is unbound.

In the good that a man or woman freely chooses is the essence of God's own goodness, the shining fulfillment of an ancient hope. Stand therefore by your resolve. Trust your innermost conscience to reveal the glow of God's desire. Plot your life by that light's course, bear steadily onward to the last, and you will have done more than you can ever know.

Along the way, make harmony your rule. By this I mean a constant determination to soothe the nerves of one's friends and foes rather than to enflame them.

Suppose an acquaintance, in a state of agitation, addresses you in less than gracious terms, charging you with an offense of which you know yourself to be perfectly innocent. How shall you respond? If your heart lacks peace and patience, the fellow's fire will catch your sleeve. Then you too will smolder and blow smoke. Suppose instead you pause and breathe. Say to yourself, this gentleman's heat is not my affair, but I am content to humor his ill temper until the truth gradually dawns, making all things clear and restoring him to proper consideration for me.

When you see that others' usage of you speaks little of your quality and much of theirs, you will be relieved of the compulsion to react in kind. A dervish was once enjoying a stroll when suddenly trumpets blared in his ears and a footman roughly thrust him aside, crying, "Clear the road!" With unruffled mien, the dervish answered, "That is why." A moment later a mounted *ghazi* approached and begged his attention, saying, "Sir, His Majesty is coming this way. I would be obliged if you would do me the favor of standing to the side." The dervish nodded and answered, "That is why." Momentarily the Sultan arrived on the back of an elephant. Glimpsing the dervish, he dismounted and silently bowed. The dervish smiled and uttered, "That is why."

Close your eyes and watch your breath. Observe first your inhalation. As you breathe in, soak up the surrounding atmosphere. Imbibe the incense of the place you inhabit. Let that fragrance, and the beings that swim in its influence, fill your body, your mind, your heart, and finally, your soul.

Hold your breath. Center yourself in your eternal nature, the changeless witness at the core of your psyche. Perceive your interior state, the disposition of your soul. As you breathe out, watch the timbre of your inner being ripple out through your heart, mind, and body, so that at last it shines through your glance and tingles in your fingertips.

Now take cognizance of the whole ebb and flow of your breath: the ingress of the world's claim upon you as you inhale and the imprint of your soul's mark as you exhale. These two movements are like to seem, at first, ill matched. But watch with patience. An unexpected sympathy will begin to show itself. The world will remain the world and your soul will remain itself, but a cord of affinity will slowly appear between the two. That cord is harmony, and it is the secret of life.

Harmony depends on tranquility, the soul's deep peace. Tranquility is the antithesis of distraction. To practice tranquility is to stand at the threshold of the infinite, accepting the necessity of action yet serenely declining to merely react.

Once Hazrat 'Ali, may God honor his face, was locked in battle with a fierce foeman. By and by the Lion of God gained the upper hand. As his enemy tumbled to the ground, 'Ali raised his arm to deliver the finishing blow. As a last gesture of defiance, the fallen warrior spat in his vanquisher's face. Instantly that august countenance flushed with heat. The offender cringed and awaited his doom. But now God's Lion sheathed his sword and walked away. Stunned, the warrior rose and pursued him, demanding to know why he had been spared. Hazrat 'Ali answered, "When you spat in my face, you piqued my ire. Anger is not a motive on which I choose to act."

Tranquility is the key to strength. The hand that emotion shakes is like to miss its mark. Prowess flows from calm nerves and stern mettle. Do not trust yourself, my son, when your blood is aboil. When your heart rattles in your breast and your breath is shallow and quick, sheathe your sword and hold your tongue. Fight, or sue for peace, another hour.

When you are firm in faith and tranquil of soul, your aim will be true, your tongue will be silver, and all that you put your mind to you will carry out with effortless aplomb. You will neither need nor expect tender mercies from the world, and when fortune beleaguers you, you will bear its slings and arrows with unfailing good cheer.

If you would attain true tranquility make yourself a force of nature. See how the earth accepts the refuse that men heap on its back, and how the ocean ungrudgingly laps up the bitterest poisons. The sky has room for all and everything, and somehow its purity remains. The elements know the meaning of fortitude, for they have been here since the beginning. So too have you, if you only knew. In that knowledge is the root of endurance.

You have heard, perhaps, of Sultan Ibrahim Adham, the king who forsook his throne to search for the Real. After years of wandering he found Shaykh Fuzayl ibn 'Ayaz and knew that he had found his master. The sheikh accepted him into his circle, but soon discovered in him a lingering trace of royal arrogance. To purge him of this vice, faint though it was, he required him to carry out the rubbish in a basket each day. One day, as Ibrahim went about his task, the sheikh instructed another disciple to overturn his burden. Ibrahim uttered a word of rebuke, but then, remembering himself, refilled the basket and went on his way. Some time later the sheikh again ordered the basket knocked down. This time Ibrahim held his tongue, though he gave the offender a chilly look. Hearing this, the sheikh gently shook his head. After some time the sheikh repeated the test. Now Ibrahim did not even look at the troublemaker. He simply knelt and collected the scattered contents of the basket. When the sheikh was informed of this, tears filled his eyes, and he named Ibrahim his successor.

Ibn Gahmuret, your soul's quest commenced at the beginning of time and will not reach its fated conclusion until time's end. Between the origin and the goal you will be shown all manner of things. All that you shall see shall have been shown to you because it must be shown. It is all the showing forth of the Real, and the Real cannot be other than she is, for indeed, the Real is all that is. Therefore, be content and learn to love destiny. Heed the wise Dhu'n-Nun, who observed, "Satisfaction is the heart's calm amid the flux of fate."

Contentment breeds a certain reserve, an easy gravity. The friend of destiny does not succumb to the weather of every passing thought-cloud that disturbs the sky of his mind. A sentinel stands between his passions and his actions. That sentinel is his serene mastery, his smooth self-possession. It will not countenance any dearth of graciousness or finesse. Though his thirst may be dry as the Sahara, he will not drink the cup before him unless and until it is to be drunk.

The wise know the wisdom of moderation. As health of body depends on the balance of the humors, a wholesome life demands balance in one's habits and pursuits. All is good in moderation and evil when taken to an extreme. In the absence of due proportion, openhandedness becomes extravagance, interest turns to interference, valor is reduced to foolhardiness, and purity devolves into prudery.

As wisdom advances, a love of simplicity grows. Luxuries lose their glamour and one learns to obtain the most satisfying pleasure from the humblest things. The ground below, the sky above, and the trees swaying in the breeze become the accoutrements of an otherworldly bliss. Then, as Hazrat 'Ali said, "He who eats wheaten bread, drinks the water of the Euphrates, and rests in the shade, that one is in Paradise."

When fantastic manias and vain caprices have been set aside in favor of life's simple pleasures, the cosmic order invariably consents to communicate its wonders. The lovesick spinning of the stars and planets, the annual pageantry of the four seasons, the soaring migrations of feathered flocks, the rhythm of the churning tide where land meets sea and the moon holds reign—these and a million other intimations of a harmony beyond human reckoning offer their voice to the music of one's passage through the earth.

On Generosity

FILS du roi Gahmuret, the whole mystic doctrine of largesse may be summed up in these simple words: at day's end, what you have given is what you have.

You will not attain beneficence until you expend of what you love.

See how scripture upsets the law of the land, the almighty rule of self-interest! Conventional wisdom instructs one to cling jealously to every inch of the property and privilege one manages to acquire. For the multitude, wealth and wellbeing are two names for the same coveted prize. But revelation urges a different logic. Since all is God's, possession is mere illusion. Yes, one may succeed in obtaining, for a time, the use of soft and glittery things. But earthly pleasures are pale and fleeting wisps. When they fly they are fled, and only their lack remains. What lasts is kindness.

Amongst the Arabs, largesse has a name. That name is Hatim Ta'i. Sir Hatim was a distinguished Yemenite gentleman of the era directly preceding the birth of our Prophet. In generosity he had no equal.

Hear how he won his wife. When Hatim's thoughts turned to matrimony, he determined to attain the hand of Mawiya Tamima, whose peerless beauty and virtue were the talk of the land. When he made bold to present himself at the maiden's residence, he discovered that he was not alone in his hopes, for a crowd of suitors stood suppliant before the door, each more lovestruck than the last. Mawiya soon appeared, bidding her admirers to be her father's guests and requesting each to compose a poem describing the purity of his blood and the excellence of his character.

When the suitors retired, Mawiya ordered a servant to slaughter a camel and distribute its meat equally among them. This done, she cleverly disguised herself as a beggar and went door-to-door pleading for a morsel to eat. One suitor gave her the camel's tail, another the liver, and a third tossed her a piece of spleen. When she came to Hatim's door she met with an entirely different reception. Hatim warmly saluted her and treated her to best of what he had.

The next day the wooers recited their poems. Mawiya listened politely and offered modest words of praise. She then ordered the servants to serve a fitting meal. As the dishes were placed before the guests and uncovered, expressions of shock and dismay filled the room. Before each suitor was that part of the camel he had given to the beggar, cooked to perfection! The shame-stricken suitors saw no recourse but to beat a hasty retreat. Only Hatim Ta'i remained. Mawiya had found her husband.

My son, it may be that in the hereafter we will be served with precisely that which we served others here on earth.

Allied with Mawiya, Hatim's affairs prospered. As his fortune soared his humility and kindness only increased. Before long his fame as a man of singular munificence spread across Arabia. The Sultan of Yemen at first took pleasure in hearing of his bounty. As a proud philanthropist, tales of charity interested him. The thought of Hatim spurred him on to give grander, more sumptuous banquets than ever before. But what was this now? His guests were cheering his liberality with comparisons to Hatim.

Stung to rage, the Sultan summoned a notorious ruffian and promised him a princely sum for Hatim's head. When the assassin reached the province of the Banu Tayy, a young man of surpassingly radiant and smiling mien greeted him with utmost courtesy and urged him to be his guest. The overwhelmed assassin followed him to his modest home, where he was regaled with every rite of hospitality. As the night progressed, the young man presented his guest with one after another choice dainty or refreshing drink.

At last, when dawn broke, the assassin recalled his mission and begged leave to go, his eyes brimming with tears of gratitude and affection. The young man remonstrated that he should stay, but the assassin would impose himself no longer. The young host begged at least to know his quest, in case he might be of assistance. Convinced of the young man's friendship, the ruffian confessed that he was a poor man who earned his bread by less than laudable means. The Sultan had hired him to kill Hatim Ta'i, and so must he do. If the young man would help him, he would be greatly obliged.

Hearing these words, without a flicker of fear, the young host proclaimed himself the very same Hatim, and presented his neck for the assassin's satisfaction.

What could the ruffian say? He dropped to the ground and kissed Hatim's feet, utterly renouncing his criminal mission. When the Sultan later heard what had befallen, he too was moved to awe and repentance.

Sir Hatim's generosity continued even after his death. The day after his body was interred, a band of weary travelers stopped and encamped at his tomb. Having exhausted their provisions, they brooded gloomily over their aching bellies and bleak prospects. Their leader, a certain Abu'l-Bukhturi, began to supplicate the late Hatim, insisting that he make good on his sterling reputation for hospitality. Suddenly one of the band's best camels lurched and keeled over. The travelers now had meat for dinner, but Abu'l-Bukhturi was not heartened. He had lost a good camel. Hatim Ta'i, he irritably observed, was very generous with *other* people's chattels.

In the morning, as the well-fed travelers prepared to depart, a dust cloud burst upon them. From its folds appeared a handsome young man leading a two-humped camel of spectacular aspect. Close inspection established the gentleman's identity as 'Adi, son of Hatim Ta'i. 'Adi politely asked for Abu'l-Bukhturi, and being shown the chief, embraced him with endearing warmth. He related that his father had come to him in a dream that night, explaining that guests had arrived. To feed them it had been necessary to borrow a camel from Abu'l-Bukhturi. Hatim therefore asked 'Adi to take a prize camel to his tomb to repay his debt. He wanted 'Adi to express his apologies for any inconvenience suffered. Conveying this, 'Adi presented the camel, the likes of which the travelers had never seen, and returned whither he had come, leaving Abu'l-Bukhturi at once elated and humbled.

As it lay in a gully, Hatim's tomb was vulnerable to the ravages of floodwater. After a strong deluge nearly washed the sepulcher away, 'Adi decided to have his father's remains disinterred and reburied in a more suitable place. When they dug up his grave, they found that his body had decomposed completely, with the exception of one extremity. His right hand, so famed for its openness, was as sound as ever! So does generosity immortalize its instrument.

Ibn Gahmuret, I would have you take a page from good Hatim's book. Be at the service of your guest, and of all who seek the shade of your kindness. Leave no one disappointed in the compass of your charity. Be generous not only with your property, but also with your solicitude. Treat every one of God's creatures with the courtesy, forbearance, and benevolence you would show to a bosom friend and comrade-in-arms. Do not withhold from the meanest of men the glance of your consideration.

In advising this line of conduct, my son, in truth I ask of you no sacrifice, for unless it is well spent, wealth is dire poverty. Quoth the saintly ad-Daqqaq of Khorasan, "Generosity is not the rich giving to the poor. In reality, it is the poor giving to the rich."

On Justice

FILS du roi Gahmuret, when I am no more, and you are of age, you will assume your rightful seat on the lion-flanked throne of Zazamanc. Your name will be pronounced in the Grand Mosque of Patelamunt, and the ruby crown of the Hakimids will be raised to your head. Though I shall be absent from your coronation in body, if God wills I shall be witness in spirit.

The holy book of Zardusht, peace be upon him, is said to tell of a wondrous nimbus that invests righteous kings and queens with a hallowed glory descended from the stars. Whenever a monarch strays from the path of mercy and justice, its mantle flees from him in the shape of a bird, leaving him bereft of honor. So did the great Jamshid fall from grace to wander for long years in ignominy.

Kingship is a demanding and perilous affair, my son. One who would venture to accept responsibility for protecting and prospering an entire kingdom must practice consummate vigilance, evenhandedness, foresight, and determination. In short, he—or, if a queen, she—must stand perpetually in the glow of heaven's beams.

As many lives as fall within the sphere of one's influence, so fateful are one's choices. A king or queen's duty is therefore of almost unequaled weight. Only the friends of God carry a heavier burden. I speak of the saints, on whose perfumed prayers the world floats.

The saints govern the invisible realm. Your destined rule concerns the world of appearances. Still, if you would fulfill the trust of your throne, you must make the ordinances of the saints your own canon. You must live and move in unbroken remembrance of the Real, and serve the truth with every word and gesture.

Arrogance is the ruin of kings. Monarchs who gloat in their might lose the sanction of heaven and the love of their people. Corrupted by power's slow poison, they scoff at the dictates of justice until divine justice overtakes them. Then their fleeting gaiety turns to enduring despair.

If you would be spared the fate of these wretches, may God forgive them, never forget yourself. Invoke the Real morning and evening, while sitting and while walking, while standing and while lying down. Remember, when you hold the scepter of sovereignty, that you and your subjects are alike God's mortal creatures. He is *Lord of all the worlds*. Such authority as you may possess is only by his leave. Do not abuse his favor.

Keep schemers and flatterers far from your ear. Surround yourself with counselors famed for moderation and foresight. Consider their advice attentively, but in the end, act on your own best lights and hold yourself to account. Shape your policies with a view to the peace and prosperity of the whole breadth of your kingdom. The nobles may people your court, but the peasantry is the foundation of a realm. Do not bar the humblest voice from the circle of your deliberations. The measure of a ruler's success is the happiness of the lowliest of her subjects.

When you mount the Leonine Throne, the swords of the army and the axe of the executioner will swish and sting at your command. Here rests your gravest trust. Force is permissible in defense of the kingdom's peace, but unwarranted bloodshed is the worst of enormities. Heed the warning words of Hazrat 'Ali, may God honor his face: "There is nothing more inviting of retribution, more momentous in consequence, more deserving of the withdrawal of blessings and the interruption of one's span of days, than the unjust shedding of blood."

Sometimes a tyrant's oppression is cut short by revolution or invasion. Just as often, despots reign interminably, multiplying their iniquities and grinding their weary subjects into the dust. Alas, such is the grim truth of the world: the brutal prosper by their brutality while the innocent suffer by their innocence.

Ambition knows no restraint. It seizes every advantage, caring nothing for honor and less for the protestations of the downfallen on whose backs it blithely treads. The law of self-interest, ruthlessly applied, can speed an egoist an untold distance on the path of power and privilege. Meanwhile the chivalrous youth lags distantly behind, murmuring at each bottleneck in the lane, "After you..."

But the wicked will not always flourish, nor will the good always languish. As 'Isa, peace be upon him, has foretold, "The first shall be last and the last first."

If in this world vice gains glory and virtue earns nothing but hardship, in the next world the tables will be turned. The mightiest tyrant will discover himself a lowly suppliant of God's forgiveness, while the poorest of his subjects—those, leastways, who were true to the truth—will be laurelled with the fragrant benedictions of paradise.

My son, keep the Day of Judgment always before your mind's eye. On that day, everything will be made clear and nothing will remain hidden. There will be no room for pretense on *the day their tongues and hands and feet bear witness to what they had done.*

Therefore, be patient. Strive continuously for justice, but know that the justice that earth cannot supply, heaven will provide. When someone offends against you, do not take offense. If he has acted unjustly it is he who will be called to account in the Sequel, not you. The injustice he has done is to his own self. So long as you guard your innocence you cannot be harmed. Yes, your worldly affairs may be impeded. You may even be injured bodily—even to the point of death. But if you have kept God's pleasure, you will have lost nothing that cannot be honorably lost.

The wise Diyujanis was once informed that a man had sworn to kill him. His only comment was, "It will do him more harm than it will me."

Do not brood over the wrongs that have been done to you, nor seek the cold solace of revenge. Pray, instead, for the souls who wrong themselves by wronging you. They stand in need of your prayers.

On Nobility

*F*ILS *du roi* Gahmuret, none but you shall determine who you are to become. Fate will apportion you circumstances, but circumstances do not make a man. You shall be known, not by fate's call, but by your answer. Let that answer be noble and you will have won the heart of your Creator, for as the holy Prophet, peace and blessings be upon him, relates, "God is beautiful and loves beauty."

Shall the recompense for grace be other than grace?

In all of your transactions, therefore, strive for beauty of manner. Never rest complacent; always seek further refinement. When you are provoked, do not regard your antagonist's conduct as justification for the taking of liberties. On the contrary, consider yourself then as put to the test, and cleave to the strict requirements of chivalry.

Speech is a potent instrument. Use it with care, or keep your own counsel. A lie stains the tongue that speaks it; the truth is pure and delicious. Speak the truth at all times, whatever the cost to your hopes. But do not confuse truth and opinion. When truth is hammered into the shape of a weapon, it is no longer truth.

You are right to claim what is yours, but claim not a jot more. Satisfy yourself with what you have been given and what you have earned. Though it may be in your power to take more, it cannot be just, and all accounts will one day be squared, down to the last dirham.

In this world so rife with perfidy and intrigue, it is no mean thing to be reckoned dependable. Better to suffer any loss than to lose the trust of those who put their faith in you. Be faithful, and conduct your affairs irreproachably.

Do not lift yourself up by casting another down. Be the author of no man's misery. If you may prosper yourself by prospering others, by all means pursue your fortune. But if your glory must come at the price of others' ruin, fie on such success! A thousand times better is honest poverty and obscurity.

There are many in this world for whom fate has proven an indifferent patron. Some are weak of limb, others slow of wit. Such men and women make easy prey for wolves and jackals. Constitute yourself their friend and protector. For your own part, never take advantage of weakness or ignorance, even in an adversary.

Have you watched children at play? Have you seen how an older sends a younger child on an errand of mischief only to slink away grinning when the guileless babe is caught in the act? Heaven allows such trickery in children, but cannot bless it in grown men and women. The bidding of a wrong is as wrong as its doing.

It is the habit of lazy and querulous minds to rush to unjust judgments. A jaundiced gaze does not see what it sees but what it fancies it sees. A Moslem meets a Christian and is convinced he stands before an unwashed barbarian. A Christian beholds a Moslem and imagines she confronts a worshipper of devils. If the two would manage to converse, and would stretch out their conversation over a succession of days, they might at last see beyond their preconceptions. How much better it would have been had they had none in the first place! As the Franks say, *Honi soit qui mal y pense*. An open mind is the posture of wisdom.

Does it not jangle your nerves to hear a person sounding the trumpet of his own praise? If it does, you will perceive the necessity of refraining from such a gaucherie. Avoid all bluster and rodomontade. Let your deeds speak for themselves.

If your worth is insufficiently valued, do not fret: *God is aware of the secrets of the hearts*. If your worth is seen and esteemed, recall your feet of clay. Return the respect of the one who respects you, and treat each and all with courtesy. When you perform a kindness, perform it quietly and forget it quickly.

There is a fine line between noble knight-errantry and officious meddling; be wary of crossing it. Offer your services only when they are wanted. Proffer your advice only on request, and then only sparingly—parental counsel being the exception!

And yet do not be stingy with your assistance. Whenever your aid is required, whoever asks it of you, do not be slow to oblige. Do not consider it a favor on your part. Rather, count it as a favor to yourself to be called upon to render needed help.

When speaking of an absent person, speak as you would speak were he or she standing before you, weighing your words. Such words as you lack the candor to put before the person concerned may not be worthily offered anywhere. *Indeed God is all-hearing and all-seeing.*

Nor is it noble to listen to slander. Imam Hasan, may God bless and keep him, relates that when a certain man was defaming another, his father Hazrat 'Ali, may God honor his face, advised him to close his ears, saying, "The fellow is only ransacking his wallet for the most worthless contents, that he may empty them into yours."

In the grip of anger, keep a tight hold on the rein of your tongue. To hurl a charge is to commit oneself. Are you certain that the one you would rebuke is truly in the wrong? Is it not possible that appearances are merely against him? Perhaps his transgression is not all that it seems. Breathe. Suppose he is in the wrong. What will your reproach accomplish? Will it be a collyrium for his eyes? More probably it will be as gall and wormwood to his heart. He will only resume and redouble his offence. Words of scorn are wasted breath, and no substitute for sound policy.

Anyone can speak his mind, but it requires a keen wit to consider the thoughts and feelings of the one whom one addresses. A bit of tact goes a long way. Considerate speech calms the listener and draws forth the most thoughtful response of which she is capable.

The more sympathy with which you regard a person, the sharper your vision will become. Instead of merely seeing effects, you will begin to see causes. At last you will perceive that the person before you is as life has made him. You will understand him and forgive his trespasses. You will, as you must, go on defending yourself and others from harm at his hand, but you will pray for him with an earnest heart. A knight of purity esteems no man his enemy.

As my son and heir to the Leonine Throne, you will be raised in the lap of luxury. I would have you know that few live thus. Many make shift with the most minimal of possessions. Others groan in dire poverty, never certain from which quarter their next meal will come. Their indigence is no more their fault than our affluence is our due. Fortune is inscrutable. Keep the picture of the hovels of the poor ever before your mind and heart, and remember the words of the Prophet: "The poor are most beloved of God."

Every man and woman possesses a sphere of responsibility unique to himself or herself. One might watch over a larger sphere and another a smaller, but both are in equal measure answerable. Discern well where your sphere begins and where it ends. Within that circumference, exert yourself to the utmost in the execution of your duty. Regard your duty as a sacred trust and symbol of your devotion to the Real. Be ever cognizant of those who depend on you, and put their interests before your own.

Do not be fickle in your affections. Stand by your friends through all the vicissitudes of stormy fate. When the Trumpet of Doomsday sounds, false friends will run from each other while sincere friends seek each other out, even through fire and brimstone.

Among friendships, the bond between man and wife is like no other. One day you will meet the fair damozel who is destined to rule your heart. When you do, love her with a love of such purity it will never die, but will instead live on forever. Such a love is named *domnei*, and is a pearl of the greatest price.

There is no feature so disagreeable as a frown, and none so agreeable as a smile. The loveliest and most irresistible of smiles is the smile that blooms in the throes of hardship. Let such a smile merely appear and misery will know itself beaten.

Faith that has not been battered by fear, harassed by doubt, and lured by temptation, and all the while shown the unbending staunchness of its mettle, is not yet faith. To hold to one's principles in prosperity is no difficult feat. Adversity is what makes or breaks a man or woman's character. Faithfulness comes easily when the fidelity costs nothing, but when its price is your wealth, your name, or your very lifeblood, will you choose it?

Nothing in this world is more precious than honor. By honor I do not mean people's opinion of you. I mean, rather, God's pleasure in you. Honor is the honest conviction that one's course of life and action conforms scrupulously to the mold of ideals revealed and illuminated by contemplation of God's nature.

When one gives one's word one gives over a part of one's soul. Do not swear an oath lightly, my son. To break a promise is a thing never ever to be thought of.

Now and again, a friend may confide a secret in you. Your friend trusts you not to disclose it. Do not let any inducement tempt you to reveal it. The silence of what should not be said is golden.

From time to time you will require assistance. If your friends are true friends, they will gladly lend their aid, though you must take care not to overtax their kindness. Do not beg a favor of one who will not grant it you. To do so is to court humiliation.

If mutual assistance is one face of life, competition is another. In swordplay, polo, and chess, belligerence is a virtue. But a challenge is only as honorable as it is fair. To confront a seasoned swordsman may be an act of fine courage, but to throw a gauntlet before an untried stripling is to proclaim oneself a bully.

In these pages I have urged you forward on the path of perfection. I freely confess that I am not, and have never been, perfect. I have stumbled and fallen more often than I wish to recall. But I have always lifted myself up and pressed on. And so must you when you fall. Never succumb to hopelessness. Draw the sword of your will and march onward toward your destiny, however foreboding the prospect ahead.

Remember the words of the divine Imam Aflatun, may God bless him: "Do good though you gain nothing but trouble from it, for the trouble will pass away and the good will endure." Nobility is its own reward.

On the Cup
Mixed With Camphor

FILS du roi Gahmuret, picture the garden of Iram on a summer night. Fallen arches and cyclopean pillars bear mute witness to the architectural reveries of an antediluvian race. Only the susurration of the breeze and the warbled plaint of a nightingale ruffle the quietude of midnight. For time out of mind Iram has known no caretaker but Nature. Still the hedges are bejeweled with rose and jasmine, and a delicate perfume mists the desert air. At the center of the garden rests a tank of crystal water awhirl with silver fish. Look into its tremulous mirror and you will see your reflection, crowned with lotus blossoms and stars. But look closer.

The face on the water is not your face. No, it is truer than your face, more faithful to the lineaments of your soul.

Spread out behind your transfigured face is another Iram. Look and see. For all its ravishing beauty, the garden in which you stand wears a worn and pallid aspect by contrast. For the moon in that other garden is no mere object of astronomy. She gazes down on you with as searching a look as the look in your own astonished eye. Yes, the moon is an angel, and as your glance surveys the moonlit panorama, angelic lights unveil themselves wherever your vision rests. Every stone, tree and dewdrop throbs with breath, inhaling life from the Unseen and exhaling orisons to the glory of the Real.

In that Iram is a tank bearing in its mirror the reflection of still another garden. Words would fail me should I try to describe it, for its splendors defy description. Summon before your mind the most breathtaking scenes of enchantment you have ever set eyes on and you will glean the merest inkling of this paradise of infinite vistas, astral flowers, emerald columns, and zephyrs fresh-blown from the Sigh of the Merciful.

Here too is a tank, and in it another garden. In that garden is the image of another, within which is another, containing still another, and so on in dazzling succession, until the ladder of gardens, each more sublime and exhilarating than the last, reaches its dizzying pinnacle at the celestial tank known as Kauthar. The face in its water is the face of the Real. To meet the gaze of that face is to be swept into the luminous gulf of eternity.

The angels who attend Kauthar have in their keeping a chalice. The Franks know this chalice as the Saint Graal. At moments of the purest exaltation faithful souls in quest of truth are given to drink from it.

Surely the righteous shall drink of a cup whose mixture is camphor.

If you would taste of this cup, my son, omit no rite of the religion of love. With each thought, word and step, rise higher on love's aery path. Scan every shape and form for beauty's trace until *whithersoever you turn, there is the Face of God.* Befall what may, do not turn aside, and when ceaseless devotion has transported you from self-possession to oblivion and back again, and your heart has been shattered and made whole again, you will become as new, as one reborn, a child of the moment. Then the rim of the cup mixed with camphor will be lifted to your lips, and you will taste the love that God bore for you even ere your soul knew life.

.

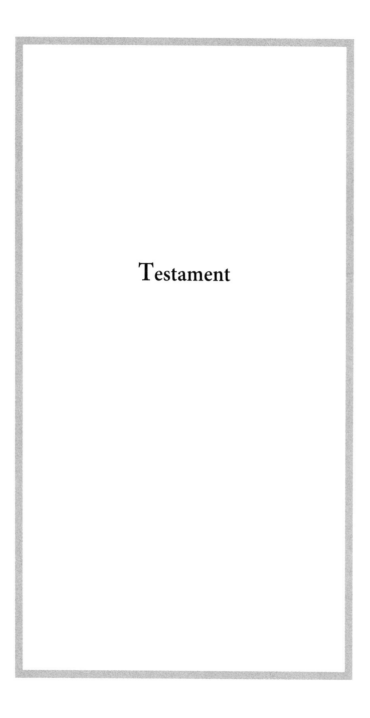

Testament

My beloved son, *fils du roi* Gahmuret, Feirefiz the Angevin, al-Hakimi, thou marvelous zebra among men, son of the Occident and the Orient, heir of the wide world!

The ink of my life is fast fading. Soon I must put down my pen and ready myself for a long sleep. I pray that, when I am wakened at the Gathering, you and your father will be at my side. Until then I shall dream of you.

No news of Ibn Gandin has reached me since his going. When you come of age, I urge you to set out for Anjou. If you fail to find your father, you may yet find kinsmen whose acquaintance is worth the making. I have a notion that destiny awaits you there.

The world is in tumult. From Iberia to the Levant, Jews, Christians and Moslems are locked in ruthless and senseless contention. The streets of the City of Peace are stained with blood.

Ibrahim, peace be upon him, is the father of all of us. If it be within your means, make common cause with the chivalry of Christendom and call the People of the Book to brotherhood and sisterhood in the shade of his ancient oak.

I pray for you every blessing, my son. May the Exalted Lord initiate you in the sweetest of mysteries and unveil to you the brightest of secrets! May you live happily, love devotedly, serve faithfully, die honorably, and return to your Lord *well-pleased and well-pleasing!*

Notes and Sources

Introduction

"A grief to Saracens"; "perfection of Paradise, both root and branch"; "like a parchment with writing all over it, black and white all mixed up"; "these pure men without flaw each bore the heart of the other, and in their strangeness to each other they were still intimate enough." Wolfram von Eschenbach, *Parzival: A Romance of the Middle Ages*, trans. Helen T. Mustard and Charles E. Passage (New York: Vintage Books, 1961), pp. 61, 129, 390, 385.

A Note on Pronouns

"If anyone asks how the feminine pronoun (*hiyya*) can bear a likeness to God, the answer is that on the Night of the Ascension, the emanations of God the Glorified and Exalted that appeared to the Lord of the World, peace and blessings be upon him, were in feminine form." Sayyid Muhammad Husayni Gisudaraz, *Wujud al-'ashiqin* (Muradabad: Matba'-yi Gulzar, 1891), p. 11.

Preamble

"Do not bring me your genealogies; bring me your actions." Ahmad ibn Abi Ya'qub Ya'qubi, *Tarikh-i Ya'qubi* (Beirut: Dar Sadir, 1960), vol. 2, p. 110.

Chapter I

Am I not your Lord? ... Yes, we testify. Qur'an 7:172. Arberry, Arthur J., trans., *The Koran Interpreted* (Oxford: Oxford University Press, 1964).

Remember him when you stand, when you sit, and when you lie down. Based on Qur'an 3:191.

Wherever you turn your face, know that he is facing you. Based on Qur'an 2:115.

Your glance never reaches him, but he reaches your glance, and all glances. Based on Qur'an 6:103.

She is closer to you than your jugular vein. Based on Qur'an 50:16.

Were it not for him, God would not have created the heavens and the earth. Based on the Hadith Qudsi, "But for you I would not have created the spheres."

Muhammad was a prophet when Adam was still between water and clay. Based on the Hadith, "I was a prophet while Adam was still between water and clay."

Not stingy of the Unseen. Qur'an 81:24 (Arberry, modified).

If all of the trees became pens and all the oceans turned to ink, still revelation would not be exhausted. Based on Qur'an 31:27.

"His character was the Koran." Hadith.

Chapter II

Do not despair of God's mercy; surely he forgives sins altogether. Qur'an 39:53 (Arberry).

"Pray as if you see God, and if you do not, know that God sees you." Hadith.

Contemplate your purity until you are united in spirit with all that is holy. ... Visualize everything crumbling to dust but her Face. Based on Sayyid Muhammad Husayni Gisudaraz, *Risala-yi muraqaba* in *Majmu'a-yi yazda rasa'il* (Hyderabad: Intizami Press, 1941), pp. 2–7 *passim*.

Chapter III

"Cast your bread upon the waters ... you cannot understand the work of God, the maker of all things." Ecclesiastes 11:1-5.

"All of it is left *except* the neck." Shaykh Muhammad ibn al-Husayn as-Sulami, *al-Futuwwa* (Amman: Dar ar-Razi, 2002), p. 16.

"Alms fall into the hand of God, the honored and glorified, before they fall into the hand of the suppliant who receives them"; "When a servant of God performs a good deed in secret, God will inscribe it in secret; if he reveals it, it will be transferred from the register of secret deeds to that of public ones; if he speaks about it, it will be removed from both registers and inscribed in the book of hypocrisy." Shaykh Abu Hamid Muhammad al-Ghazali, *Ihya' 'ulum al-din* (Beirut: Dar Sadir, 2010), vol. 1, pp. 291, 289.

Chapter IV

"Five things break the fast: deceit, slander, tale-bearing, perjury, and covetous glances." Al-Ghazali, vol. 1, p. 314.

Eat and drink, and be at peace. If you see any man, tell him: "I have verily vowed a fast to the All-merciful and cannot speak to any one today." Qur'an 19:26. Ali, Ahmed, trans., *Al-Qur'an* (Princeton: Princeton University Press, 1984), modified.

"The proper answer to a fool is silence." Maulana Jalal al-Din Muhammad Balkhi, *Masnavi-yi ma'navi* (Tehran [?]: Intisharat-i Bihnud, 1954), p. 531.

"The fast is for me, and I am the reward that comes with it." Hadith Qudsi.

Chapter V

God does not burden a soul beyond capacity. Qur'an 2:286 (Ahmed Ali).

Man took it on himself. Qur'an 33:72 (Ahmed Ali).

I have shaped him, and breathed my spirit in him. Qur'an 15:29 (Arberry).

Chapter VI

Strive in the way of God with a service worthy of him. Qur'an 22:78 (Ahmed Ali).

If God had not restrained some men through some others, monasteries, churches, synagogues, and mosques, where the name of God is honored most, would have been razed. Qur'an 22:40 (Ahmed Ali).

Killing a human is like killing humanity, and saving one is like saving it. Based on Qur'an 5:32.

"Fear God in your treatment of animals." Hadith.

If they are inclined toward peace, make peace with them, and have trust in God. Qur'an 8:61 (Ahmed Ali).

Truly with hardship comes ease. Qur'an 94:5 (Arberry).

Chapter VII

"The servant's struggle against his lust." Hadith.

Say, the spirit is of the bidding of my Lord. Qur'an 17:85 (Arberry).

The self commands one to evil, unless my Lord have mercy. Qur'an 12:53 (Ahmed Ali, modified).

Blaming self. Qur'an 75:2.

We have honored the children of Adam. Qur'an 17:70 (Ahmed Ali).

Every day in new splendor he shines. Qur'an 55:29. Abdullah Yusuf Ali, trans., *The Holy Qur'an* (Lahore: Sh. Muhammad Ashraf, 1973), modified.

"Take notice! If you wish, I will endow you with all of the pleasures of the world, but I will remove concern for me from your heart, for such concern and the pleasures of the world cannot abide together in one heart." Shaykh Farid ad-Din 'Attar Nishaburi, *Tazkirat al-awliya'* (Tehran: Bihzad, 1994/95), p. 100.

Its eyes do not swerve nor sweep astray. Based on Qur'an 53:17.

What is to come is better for you than what has gone before. Qur'an 93:4 (Ahmed Ali).

O you tranquil self, return to your Lord, well-pleased and well-pleasing! Enter then among my votaries; enter then my garden! Qur'an 89:27–30 (Ahmed Ali, modified).

Chapter VIII

Say 'God.' Then leave them alone, playing their game of plunging. Qur'an 6:91 (Arberry).

No reproach this day shall be on you; God will forgive you; he is the most merciful of the merciful. Qur'an 12:92 (Arberry).

"The chivalrous youth is one who has no enemies." Shaykh 'Abd al-Karim ibn Hawazin al-Qushayri, *ar-Risala al-Qushayriya* (Cairo: Muhammad 'Ali Subayh, 1966), p. 177.

Meeting of the two seas ... this is what we were seeking! Qur'an 18:60-64 (Arberry).

A messenger from themselves. Qur'an 3:164 (Arberry).

They did not slay him, neither crucified him, only a likeness of that was shown them. ... God raised him up to him; God is all-mighty, all-wise. Qur'an 4:157-58 (Arberry).

"The most chivalrous of you is 'Ali"; "a nobility which ennobles the valorous and generous"; "He is of me and I am of him." Shaykh Husayn Va'iz Kashifi, *Futuwwat-nama-yi sultani* (Tehran: Bunyad-i Far-hang-i Iran, 1971), pp. 19-20.

Eight rules there are that you must observe when your father's sword is yours. ... If a sheath is lacking, cover it with a cloth. Based on Kashifi, p. 353.

"The salt of the earth," Matthew 5:13.

Surely the pious shall drink of a cup whose mixture is camphor ... for we fear from our Lord a frowning day, inauspicious.' Qur'an 76:6–10 (Arberry, modified).

Chapter IX

I was a hidden treasure and I longed to be known, so I created the world that I might be known. Hadith Qudsi.

"Who knows himself knows his Lord." Hadith.

"O Lord, whenever I heed the voices of the beasts, the rustle of the trees, the purl of the waters, the songs of the birds, the delight of the shade, the roar of the wind, or the rumble of thunder, I find in them testimony to your unity." Shaykh Abu Nu'aym al-Isba-hani, *Hilyat al-awliya' wa tabaqat al-asfiya'* (Beirut: Dar al-Kitab al-'Arabi, 1967–68), vol. 9, p. 342.

You behold the earth blackened, then, when we send down water upon it, it quivers, and swells, and puts forth herbs of every joyous kind. Qur'an 22:5 (Arberry, modified).

"Love is a fire; when it befalls the heart, it burns away all but the well-beloved." Cf. al-Qushayri, p. 251, and Balkhi, p. 645.

It is he who made the sun a radiance, and the moon a light. Qur'an 10:5 (Arberry).

"Qualify yourself with the qualities of Allah." Hadith.

Ya Rabb fahhim li, ya Hu. Sayyid Muhammad Husayni Gisudaraz, *Azkar-i Chishtiyya* in *Majmu'a-yi yazda rasa'il* (Hyderabad: Intizami Press, 1941), p. 12.

Chapter X

Do you not see the birds held high between the heavens and the earth? Nothing holds them but God. Qur'an 16:79 (Ahmed Ali, modified).

He is with you wherever you are. Qur'an 57:4 (Arberry).

"If this cup may not pass away from me, except I drink it, your will be done!" Matthew 26:42.

"I shall die today"; "I have prayed to God to re-unite you with me, as first of my house, and to place you beside me"; "The Highest Friend!"; "Prayer! Prayer! You shall hold together so long as you pray together. Prayer! Prayer!" Al-Ghazali, vol. 5, p. 221.

"I am victorious, by the Lord of the Ka'ba!" Ibid, vol. 5, p. 229.

Do not say of those slain in God's way, 'They are dead'; rather they are living, but you are not aware. Qur'an 2:154 (Arberry).

"O my brother! I am to attain something the likes of which I have never attained." Al-Ghazali, vol. 5, p. 229.

Chapter XI

Will you place one there who would create disorder and shed blood, while we intone your litanies and sanctify your name? ... I know what you do not know. Qur'an 2:30 (Ahmed Ali).

"When you spat in my face, you piqued my ire. Anger is not a motive on which I choose to act." Based on Balkhi, p. 153.

"Satisfaction is the heart's calm amid the flux of fate." Shaykh Abu Bakr Muhammad al-Kalabadhi, *at-Ta'arruf li-madhhab ahl at-tasawwuf* (Beirut: Dar al-Kutub 'Ilmiya, 1993), p. 120.

"He who eats wheaten bread, drinks the water of the Euphrates, and rests in the shade, that one is in Paradise." Ahmad ibn Muhammad ibn Miskawayh, *Javidan khirad*, trans. Edward Henry Palmer (unpublished MS, Cleveland Public Library), p. 100, modified.

Chapter XII

You will not attain beneficence until you expend of what you love. Qur'an 3:92 (Arberry, modified).

"Generosity is not the rich giving to the poor. In reality, it is the poor giving to the rich." Al-Qushayri, p. 196.

Chapter XIII

Lord of all the worlds. Qur'an 1:2 (Ahmed Ali).

"There is nothing more inviting of retribution, more momentous in consequence, more deserving of the withdrawal of blessings and the interruption of the one's span of days, than the unjust shedding of blood." Imam 'Ali ibn Abi Talib, *Nahj al-balagha* (Beirut: Mu'assasat al-Ma'arif, 1990), p. 646.

"The last will be first, and the first will be last." Matthew 20:16.

The day their tongues and hands and feet bear witness to what they had done. Qur'an 24:24 (Ahmed Ali).

"It will do him more harm than it will me." Ibn Miskawaykh, p. 228.

Chapter XIV

"God is beautiful and loves beauty." Hadith.

Shall the recompense for grace be other than grace? Qur'an 55:60 (Arberry, modified).

God is aware of the secrets of the hearts. Qur'an 3:119 (Ahmed Ali).

Indeed God is all-hearing and all-seeing. Qur'an 22:75 (Ahmed Ali, modified).

"The fellow is only ransacking his wallet for the most worthless contents, that he may empty them into yours." Ibn Miskawayh, p. 106.

"The poor are most beloved of God." As-Sulami, p. 15.

"Do good though you gain nothing but trouble from it, for the trouble will pass away and the good will endure." Ibn Miskawayh, p. 187, modified.

Chapter XV

Surely the righteous shall drink of a cup whose mixture is camphor. Qur'an 76:5 (Arberry, modified).

Whithersoever you turn, there is the Face of God. Qur'an 2:115 (Arberry).

Testament

Well-pleased and well-pleasing. Qur'an 89:28 (Ahmed Ali).

Other Works Consulted

Abu Ja'far Muhammad al-Tabari. *The Caliphate of Yazid b. Mu'awiyah*. Trans. I.K.A. Howard. Albany: State University of New York Press, 1990.

Husayn Wa'iz Kashifi Sabzawari. *The Royal Book of Spiritual Chivalry*. Trans. Jay R. Crook. Chicago: Kazi Publications, 2000.

Risala-yi Hatimiya. Tehran: Chapkhana-yi Nahzat, 1941.

Imdad Allah Muhajir Makki. *Ziya' al-qulub.* Delhi: Matba'-yi Mujtaba'i, 1894.

Inayat Khan, Hazrat. *The Sufi Message.* London: Barrie and Rockliff/Jenkins, 1960–67. 13 volumes.

Kai Ka'us ibn Iskandar. *A Mirror for Princes: The Qabus Nama.* Trans. Reuben Levy. New York: E.P. Dutton, 1951.

Kalim Allah Jahanabadi, Shah. *Kashkul-i Kalimi.* Delhi: Matba'-yi Mujtaba'i, 1890–91.

Knappert, Jan. *Islamic Legends: Histories of the Heroes, Saints and Prophets of Islam.* Leiden: E.J. Brill, 1985. 2 volumes.

Muhammad bin Khavendshah bin Mahmud. *The Rauzat-us-safa or Garden of Purity.* Trans. Edward Rehatsek. Delhi: Idarah-i Adabiyat-i Delli, 1982. 5 volumes.

Nasir ad-Din Muhammad Tusi. *The Nasirean Ethics.* Trans. G.M. Wickens. London: Allen & Unwin, 1964.

Ridgeon, Lloyd. *Jawanmardi: A Sufi Code of Honour.* Edinburgh: Edinburgh University Press, 2011.

Ziya' ad-Din Nakhshabi. *Silk as-suluk.* Tehran: Kitabfarushi-yi Zavvar, 1991.

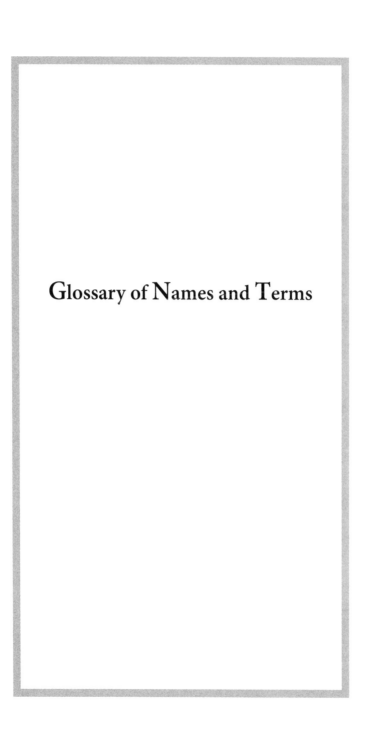

Glossary of Names and Terms

Abu Bakr al-Warraq (d. 893): an influential Sufi sheikh and author who lived and taught in Balkh.

Abu'l-Fityan: "Father of Chivalrous Youths," an honorific applied to Abraham.

Abu'l-Mihjan: a Companion of the Prophet famed for his prowess in battle.

Ad-Daqqaq (d. 1015): an ascetic of Nishapur, teacher of al-Qushayri.

Aflatun: Plato.

'A'isha (d. 678): a wife of the Prophet, and a political leader after his death.

'Ali (d. 661): cousin of the Prophet, husband of Fatima; for Sunnis, the fourth Rightly-Guided Caliph; for Shiites, the first Imam.

Anfortas: the wounded Fisher King, who guards the Grail at Munsalvaesche.

Angelica: in *Orlando Furioso*, a Cathayan princess wooed by Orlando and Rinaldo.

Angevin: of the Angevin dynasty, whose empire extended from the Pyrenees to Ireland in the 12th and early 13th centuries.

Anjou: the county surrounding Angers in the French Loire Valley.

Avesta: the primary sacred texts of the Zoroastrian religion.

Azagouc: a legendary North African kingdom, won by Gahmuret.

Azar: the Biblical Terah, father of Abraham.

Bahira: a Syrian Christian anchorite who foretold to the young Muhammad his prophetic destiny.

Banu Tayy: an Arab tribe of the Qahtanite group, based in the region of the Aja and Salma mountains.

Battle of Jaffa: the final battle of the Third Crusade, fought in 1192.

Battle of Uhud: the second battle between the pagan Meccans and the Moslems of Medina, fought in 625 beside Mount Uhud.

bel ami: beau.

Bradamante: in *Orlando Furioso*, Rinaldo's sister, a formidable knightess.

Buraq: The fabulous steed that carried the Prophet through the celestial spheres on the night of his Ascension.

Caliph: a successor of the Prophet as political leader of the Islamic community.

Charlemagne (d. 814): Charles the Great, King of the Franks and, following his conquest of Italy, Holy Roman Emperor.

Cervantes, Miguel de (d. 1616): author of the chivalric parody *Don Quixote*.

cheval: horse

Chrétien de Troyes (d. ca. 1190): a French *trouvère*, author of five Arthurian romances.

The City of Peace: *Dar as-salam*, Jerusalem.

Cœur de Lion: "Lionheart," sobriquet of Richard I.

Companions of the Cave: the fabled "Seven Sleepers" of Ephesus, whose story is told in Qur'an 18:9–26.

Cundrie: Gawain's sister, the "loathly lady" Grail messenger.

Dar al-Islam: the Islamic world.

Da'ud: the Biblical David.

Dhammapad: the Dhammapada, a Pali Buddhist scripture attributed to the Buddha.

Dhu'l-Hijjah: the twelfth month of the Islamic calendar.

Dhu'n-Nun (d. 860): a prominent early Sufi saint of Egypt, credited with knowledge of alchemy.

Diaz de Vivar, Don Rodrigo (d. 1099): a celebrated Castilian military adventurer, hero of *The Poem of the Cid*.

Diyujanis: Diogenes of Sinope.

domnei: the devotion of a knight to his lady.

El Cid: *as-sayyid*, "Lord."

Fatima: daughter of Muhammad and Khadija, wife of 'Ali, mother of Hasan and Husayn.

Feirefiz: son of Prince Gahmuret and Queen Belacane.

Filistin: Palestine.

Fils du roi: "son of king […]"; in *Parzival*, a standard appellation for princes.

fityan: "young men," spiritual knights.

Flegetanis: the Moorish astrologer from whose writings Kyot learned the story of the Grail.

futuwwa[t]: chivalry.

Fuzayl bin ʿAyaz (d. 803): a scholarly ascetic who had once been a highwayman.

Ghatsamani: Gethsemane.

ghazi: a Moslem knight.

Hahut: the transcendent plane.

Hajar: the Biblical Hagar.

Hakimids: the legendary dynasty founded by King Menelik, son of Solomon and the Queen of Sheba.

hanif: a monotheist.

Harun: the Biblical Aaron.

Harun ar-Rashid (d. 809): the fifth Abbasid caliph.

Hasan (d. 669): the elder son of ʿAli and Fatima.

Hawwa: the Biblical Eve.

Herzeloyde: Queen of Waleis, second wife of Gahmuret, mother of Parzival.

Honi soit qui mal y pense: "Shame be to him who thinks ill of it," a chivalric motto.

Hurr ibn Yazid (d. 680): an Umayyad general, commissioned with preventing Husayn and his party from entering Kufa.

Iblis: Lucifer.

ibn: in Arabic, "son of."

Ibn al-Hakim: "Son of the Wise," sobriquet of Menelik.

Ibn Muljam: a Kharijite appointed to assassinate 'Ali.

Ibrahim: the Biblical Abraham.

Ibrahim Adham (d. 777–78): a renowned ascetic.

Ilyas: the Biblical Elijah.

Imam Shafi'i (d. 820): a celebrated Moslem jurist and founder of the Shafi'i school of law.

Injil: the holy book revealed to Jesus; in the Christian tradition, the Gospels.

Iram: a lost city mentioned in Qur'an 89:7.

Iraqlitus: Heraclitus of Ephesus.

Ishaq: the Biblical Isaac.

Ishba': Elisabeth, wife of Zechariah, mother of John the Baptist.

Isma'il: the Biblical Ishmael.

Jabarut: the spiritual plane.

Jamshid: a fabled ancient Persian monarch of the Pishdadian Dynasty.

Jibra'il: the archangel Gabriel.

Ka'ba: a cubical building in Mecca of ancient and enduring sanctity.

Kauthar: a water tank in Paradise, the name of which means "abundance."

Khizr: the Green Man of Islam, guide of Moses and of numerous saints.

Al-Juljula: Golgotha.

Al-Kindi (d. 873): the first major Moslem exponent of philosophy, an Arab polymath attached to the Abbasid House of Wisdom in Baghdad.

Khumm: the pond at which the Prophet named 'Ali his spiritual successor.

Koran (Qur'an): the holy book revealed to the Prophet Muhammad.

Kufa: a city in Iraq, the capital of the caliphate under 'Ali.

Kyot: Wolfram von Eschenbach's Provençal "master," described as "laschantiure," meaning either a magician or a singer.

la ilaha illa'Llah: "there is no god but God."

La Belle Isolde: the Irish princess Iseult, heroine of the legend of Tristan and Iseult.

Lahut: the divine plane.

Malakut: the mental plane.

Muharram: the first month of the Islamic calendar.

Mahmud (d. 1030): ruler of the Ghaznavid Empire at its peak.

Makeda: Bilqis, the Biblical Queen of Sheba.

Maryam: Mary, mother of Jesus.

Munsalvaesche: the castle of the Grail, also known as Corbenic.

Musa: the Biblical Moses.

Mutawakkil (d. 890): the tenth Abbasid caliph.

Namrud: the Biblical Nimrod.

Nasut: the physical plane.

niswan: "women," spiritual knightesses.

ojalá: in Spanish, "God willing," from the Arabic *insha'Llah.*

Orlando: the hero of Boiardo's *Orlando Innamorato* and Ariosto's *Orlando Furioso.*

Palomydes: a Saracen knight of the Round Table.

Parzival: the great Grail romance of Wolfram von Eschenbach.

Parzival: the hero of Chrétien de Troyes' *Perceval* and Wolfram von Eschenbach's *Parzival.*

Patelamunt: the capital of Zazamanc.

Perceval: the unfinished fifth Arthurian romance of Chrétien de Troyes.

Prester John: a fabled oriental monarch whose kingdom was variously identified as India, Central Asia, or Ethiopia.

Reconquista: the gradual retaking of Iberia by Christian powers.

Repanse de Schoye: the Grail bearer, daughter of King Frimutel, wife of Feirefiz.

Richard I (d. 1189): King of England and leader of the Third Crusade.

Rinaldo: a knight in *Orlando Furioso*; the "Renaud de Montauben" of Old French romances.

Rizwan: the angelic doorkeeper of Paradise.

Ruggiero: in Orlando Furioso, a Saracen warrior, the son of a Christian knight and Moorish lady.

Saladin (d. 1193): Salah ad-Din Yusuf ibn Ayyub, founder of the Ayyubid Dynasty in Egypt and Syria.

Salman Pak: a Companion of the Prophet of Persian origin.

Sara: the Biblical Sarah.

Sarras: a mystical island associated with the Grail in Arthurian romances; Malory's "Spiritual Place."

Sayyid Muhammad Husayni Gisudaraz (d. 1422): a prolific Chishti saint of India, buried in Gulbarga in the Deccan.

Serendib: Ceylon.

Shibli (d. 946): a prominent Sufi of the Baghdad school.

Shim'un: Simon Peter.

Shu'ayb: the Biblical Jethro.

Suhayb ar-Rumi: a Companion of the Prophet, formerly a Byzantine slave.

subhana'Llah: "glory be to God."

Sulayman: the Biblical Solomon.

tabarruk: benediction.

tahannuth: the mystic retreat of the *hanifs*.

Tawra: the holy book revealed to Moses; in the Jewish tradition, the Torah.

Terre de Salvaesche: the kingdom surrounding Munsalvaesche.

Tristan: a knight of the Round Table and hero of the legend of Tristan and Iseult.

Tristan and Iseult: a medieval romance and tragedy extant in several versions.

Tuba Tree: a tree of Paradise alluded to in Koran 13:29.

Vedas: the most ancient collection of Indian sacred texts, composed in Sanskrit.

Vis and Ramin: an ancient Persian romance, rendered in verse in the 11ᵗʰ century by Fakhr al-Din Gurgani.

wa Allahu a'lam: "and God knows [best]."

Waleis: either Wales or Valois, a region northeast of Paris.

Wolfram von Eschenbach (d. 1220): a Bavarian knight, author of *Parzival*.

Wujud al-'ashiqin: a Persian treatise on spiritual love by Gisudaraz.

Yahya: John the Baptist.

Yazid: the second Umayyad caliph.

Ya'qub: the Biblical Jacob.

Yushua: the Biblical Joshua.

Yusuf: the Biblical Joseph

Zabur: the holy book revealed to David; in the Jewish and Christian traditions, the Psalms.

Zakariyya: Zechariah, husband of Elisabeth, father of John the Baptist.

Zamzam: a sacred well in Mecca from which pilgrims drink.

Zardusht: Zarathustra, or Zoroaster.

Zazamanc: a legendary North African kingdom.

Acknowledgements

THE author wishes to thank Shams Kairys for his thoughtful editing; Sandra Lillydahl, of the University of Massachusetts Amherst Libraries and Omega Publications, for bibliographic support and the graphic design of the book; and Ahura Burns for additional bibliographic support.

Pᴵᴿ Zia Inayat-Khan, is a scholar and teacher of Sufism in the lineage of his grandfather, Hazrat Inayat Khan. He received his B.A. (Hons) in Persian Literature from the London School of Oriental and African Studies, and his M.A. and Ph.D. in Religion from Duke University. Pir Zia is president of the Sufi Order International and founder of Suluk Academy, a school of contemplative study with branches in the United States and Europe. His first publication, the anthology *A Pearl in Wine: Essays in the Life, Music and Sufism of Hazrat Inayat Khan,* was published by Omega Publications in 2001. Together with Shaikh al-Mashaik Mahmood Khan he leads the Knighthood of Purity of the Hazrati Order.

For more information on Sufism
and the Knighthood of Purity see:

www.sufiorder.org
www.knighthoodofpurity.org

Ꮥulūk Press is an imprint of Omega Publications, Inc. Sulūk is an Arabic word meaning travel. We invite you to journey with us.

Our purpose is to unite
spirit and matter

—Pir Zia 2 Nov 2013